WALL STREET MONEY MACHINE

VOLUME 3

BULLS & BEARS

You can't get lucky if you're not in the game.
—WADE B. COOK

WALL STREET MONEY MACHINE

VOLUME 3
BULLS & BEARS

Formerly titled *Bear Market Baloney*

WADE B. COOK

Lighthouse Publishing Group, Inc.
Seattle, Washington

Lighthouse Publishing Group, Inc.
Copyright © 2000 Wade B. Cook

Library of Congress Cataloging-in-Publication Data
In Progress

"This publication is designed to provide general information in regard to the subject matter covered. It is sold with the understanding that the publisher is not engaged in rendering legal, accounting, or other professional services. If legal, accounting, or other professional services are required, the services of an independent professional should be sought."

"From a declaration of principles jointly adopted by a committee of the American Bar Association and the committee of the Publisher's Association.

Book Design by Judy Burkhalter
Dust Jacket Design by Angela Wilson
Dust Jacket and Inside Photographs by Zachary Cherry

Published by Lighthouse Publishing Group, Inc
14675 Interurban Avenue South
Seattle, Washington 98168-4664
1-800-706-8657
206-901-3100 (fax)

Source Code: WSMMV300

Printed in United States of America
10 9 8 7 6 5 4 3 2 1

To:

My wonderful son,
Benjamin,
a great kid and
a loving son.

This purple jacket is dedicated to
my lovely wife, Laura,
who loves purple.
"A wife of noble character . . .
she is worth far more than rubies, . . .
she brings her husband good, not harm,
all the days of her life, . . .
she is clothed in fine linen and purple,
she is clothed with strength and dignity,
she can laugh at the days to come and
she speaks with wisdom, . . .
her children arise and call her blessed;
her husband also, and he praises her:
Many women do noble things,
but you surpass them all.'"
From: Proverbs 31

BOOKS BY LIGHTHOUSE PUBLISHING GROUP, INC.

THE WALL STREET MONEY MACHINE SERIES, WADE B. COOK

*Wall Street Money Machine, Volume 1:
Revised And Updated For The New Millennium
Wall Street Money Machine, Volume 2: Stock Market Miracles
Wall Street Money Machine, Volume 3: Bulls & Bears*
(formerly titled Bear Market Baloney)
Wall Street Money Machine, Volume 4: Safety 1st Investing

On Track Investing, DAVID R. HEBERT
Rolling Stocks, GREGORY WITT
Sleeping Like A Baby, JOHN C. HUDELSON
Making A Living In The Stock Market, BOB ELDRIDGE

101 Ways To Buy Real Estate Without Cash, WADE COOK
Cook's Book On Creative Real Estate, WADE COOK
How To Pick Up Foreclosures, WADE COOK
Owner Financing, WADE COOK
Real Estate For Real People, WADE COOK
Real Estate Money Machine, WADE COOK

Blueprints For Success, VARIOUS AUTHORS
Brilliant Deductions, WADE B. COOK
Million Heirs, JOHN V. CHILDERS, JR.
The Secret Millionaire Guide To Nevada Corporations
JOHN V. CHILDERS, JR.
Wealth 101, WADE B. COOK

A+, WADE B. COOK
Business Buy The Bible, WADE B. COOK
Don't Set Goals (The Old Way), WADE B. COOK
Wade Cook's Power Quotes, Volume 1, WADE COOK

Living In Color, RENAE KNAPP

OTHER BOOKS BY WADE COOK

Y2K Gold Rush
GOLD LEAF PRESS

CONTENTS

PREFACE

Chance favors the informed mind.

—Louis Pasteur

T his book will not only explain my feelings about the market-place, but strategies and formulas to implement before, during, and after a small or large downturn in the market. I see so much bad news in the midst of so much downplayed good news. This news is listened to and watched by so many people that I couldn't resist writing my thoughts. With a passion I wrote, collected ideas, and put together this book. I have never acted so quickly. I wanted this information out to give hope, encouragement, and actual "how to" advice on how to prosper in these times.

One interesting side note was jockeying over the title. At first I wanted "Bear Market Baloney." Then our publications department came up with "Bear Market Bull-oney." This became the working title and I started showing the artwork around. I had to explain it every other time. Then a new title popped up: Bear "Market: Bull Money," and while I think it is extremely clever, it too must be thought out, or explained. Since there really are tried and proven ways to make real money in all types of markets I settled on a book of great cash flow strategies and added this book to my *Wall Street Money Machine* series as *Volume 3: Bulls & Bears.*

Actually, I've had to explain the term "Bear Market" to quite a few people. I was dismayed at first but encouraged later as I thought of this. There are countless people who do not know what a bull or bear market is. They have been through both, but didn't even know it. These people do not know how to play the ups and downs. This gives my company and me a great opportunity for service.

This book was originally released under the title, *Bear Market Baloney*. All the variations on the word "baloney" were clever, and meaningful in a way. But alas, I had to get back to the word that meant what I wanted the title, indeed the book, to say. Bulls and Bears: Cash flow up and down the line.

It is quite by design that this book, which does address how to make money in a bear market, is now part of my *Wall Street Money Machine* Series. Now my message is even clearer: Even in a bull market, you can still be profitable and employ the money machine concepts.

One might get the impression I'm ignoring all the news, or pointing fingers. On the contrary, I want to use this news, as misguided as it sometimes is, to build cash flow. One might think I don't believe there will ever be another bear market. That is not what I think, nor what I've written in this book.

I will say it succinctly and without disclaimer: I think we are heading toward a bear market. There, are you happy? It seems everyone wants bad news.

Yes, there will be a bear market. There have always been dips, corrections, crashes, *but a bear market is not imminent.* There is plenty of time to make some real, "big time" money in the current bull market and then thrive or excel in any downturn.

I'm projecting out one and a half to three years this new millennium, say to 2002 or 2004, and I don't see a bear market. As baby boomers get older, trade barriers diminish, taxes come down a little (or are at least held in check), the current good market could even easily continue through 2005, and even to 2008, without a 1929 or 1987 type crash.

Let's get to work. Let's keep things in perspective. Let's not give in to fear mongering by self-serving "money moguls." We don't need to put blinders on—we need to see all around us. Yes, let's get back to basics, and pick fundamentally great stocks to play. Yes, let's use aggressive strategies to build income, but use them sparingly. Yes, let's gamble on optimism. To all other negative emanations, let's just say, "Nonsense."

Optimism is a [medicine].
Pessimism is a poison.
Admittedly, every businessman must be realistic.
He must gather facts,
analyze them candidly
and strive to draw logical conclusions,
whether favorable or unfavorable.
He must not engage in self-delusion.
He must not view everything through rose-colored glasses.
Granting this, the incontestable truth is that America has
been built up by optimists.
Not by pessimists,
but by men possessing courage,
confidence in the nation's destiny,
by men willing to adventure,
to shoulder risks terrifying to the timid.

—B. C. FORBES

ACKNOWLEDGMENTS

The actions of men are like the index of a book; they point out what is most remarkable in them.

—AUTHOR UNKNOWN

No book is written or created in a vacuum. This book would not be what it is without the help of several people, Jerald Miller, Mark Engelbrecht, Angela Wilson, Judy Burkhalter, Sam Hemenway, and Brent Magarrell. I appreciate the hard work each of these people put into this book.

Laura, my faithful wife, also deserves much recognition. Without her loving support and assistance, I would not be able to do what I do. Without her optimisim and encouragement, I would not be the man that I am.

ABBREVIATIONS

Throughout this book, the author or others may refer to the names of other books or seminars. The following abbreviations may be used:

BRILLIANT DEDUCTIONS	BD
NEXT STEP SEMINAR AND/OR WORKSHOP	NS
REAL ESTATE MONEY MACHINE	REMM
STOCK MARKET MIRACLES	SMM, WSMM2
WALL STREET MONEY MACHINE	WSMM1
WALL STREET WORKSHOP™	WSWS
WEALTH INFORMATION NETWORK™	W.I.N.™

Other abbreviations that may be used:

DOW JONES INDUSTRIAL AVERAGE	DJIA, DJ-30
GENERAL AGREEMENT ON TARIFFS AND TRADES	GATT
NATIONAL ASSOCIATION OF SECURITIES DEALERS AUTOMATED QUOTATION SYSTEM	NASDAQ
NEW YORK STOCK EXCHANGE	NYSE
STANDARDS & POORS 500™	S&P 500

1

NOT NOW

Markets are currently in a state of uncertainty and flux and money is made by discounting the obvious and betting on the unexpected.

—GEORGE SOROS

I have, throughout this book, put together a collection of statements, transcriptions of public addresses, comments made in training sessions, and W.I.N.™ (Wealth Information Network™, our Internet service). My conclusions, made so often and based on different criteria at different times, have been relatively the same even as the current problem or question varied. However, the sum is a total of the parts and the parts say simply, "There will not be a bear market." Not now.

You, the reader, have a lot riding on how you perceive the market: where it's heading and how you're going to play it. To your stockbroker or financial planner (unless you find a rare one who really cares), the market going down probably will help the commission picture—there will be more people selling their positions to make commissions. But to you, it's the ham and egg example. The egg is a token donation for the chicken. The ham is "all there is" for the pig. You're in the pig's place. So, consider carefully all of the following comments and examples.

I don't think a bear market (one in the classical bear market sense) is about to happen. Might the market soften a little? Yes. Might there be temporary dips in the market and, more specifically, in a particular stock? Definitely yes.

My rationale for "not now" is not complicated and does not require a long thesis. Here it is:

1. There is no recession on the horizon.

2. Inflation is in check and the Federal Reserve is dedicated to keeping it there.

3. Corporate earnings are up everywhere. In some quarters, the only disappointing news is earnings coming in lower than what analysts expected. Ironic? Yes. Corporations are making millions, expanding sales, reducing debt, and growing; then a $160 stock falls $8 in one hour because of 2¢ less in reported earnings than was expected.

4. Taxes probably won't increase (at least directly) too much. There are too many conservatives hell-bent on lowering them to have much of a chance for increase. There might even be a capital gains tax reduction, which would be great—if only we can get some politicians to realize what a financial boon a reduction would create.

> *People's spending habits depend more on how wealthy they feel than with the actual amount of their current income.*
> —A. S. PIGOU

5. Interest rates will move up and down slightly in response to what the "Fed" perceives as inflationary.

6. Trade barriers are coming down worldwide. I don't care what your political persuasion is or how you view NAFTA and GATT (I personally don't agree with some of it, especially with some of the sovereignty issues). These agreements, with more to follow, have stimulated trade.

   a. The rest of the world needs so much of what we have. We are the world leaders in:
      - Pharmaceuticals
      - Bio-technology
      - Hi-tech computers and all the peripherals: hardware, software, content, and applications
      - Construction
      - And too many more to mention here.

   b. Way over half the world's population (some say 75% or more) are living in third world countries. Even the former Soviet Union and China qualify. There are countless "dollar-based" millionaires in these countries, and that, added to an exponentially growing middle class, bodes well for our products and services. (Note: India alone has a burgeoning middle class as large as the entire population of the United States.)

      Life is an illusion. You are what you think you are.
      —YALE HIRSCH

   c. We can invest in these foreign companies or invest in American companies expanding into these new markets.

   d. Expansion of existing products into new markets is a healthier prospect than developing new products for old markets. For example: McDonalds will do better opening up more stores in China than developing an octopus sandwich to sell in Kansas.

I'll deal with earnings more in several other places accompanied with strategies for making money, but in the theme of this Chapter, "Not Now," I'd like to add a few thoughts:

There are definitely some companies' stocks with astronomical multiples—huge price/earnings ratios. These high prices usually won't be sustained unless the actual "drop-to-the-bottom-line" profits pick up—or rise to meet the high multiples. However, across the board of NYSE, NASDAQ, and S&P 500, multiples are not that high. Are they on the high side historically? Yes, a little. Have some retreated to more conservative levels? Yes, look at bank stocks, and food stocks.

Many American companies are simply doing well. Management in most companies is in sync with customers and employees. Most are concerned with quality, which helps build a good expanding bottom line and great shareholder value. America is once again the world leader in productivity.

> *Statements by high officials are practically always*
> *misleading when they are designed to bolster a falling market.*
> —GERALD LOEB

When companies' multiples get really low, they become turnaround candidates and takeover/merger candidates. Many companies are on the prowl for new businesses, which can add immediate earnings to their own bottom line.

Add all of this to the fact that so much of the world lies within reach and we have a triple whammy:

1. Low inflation

2. No recession

3. Good corporate earnings.

So, when will a bear market occur? I'm not a prognosticator. I don't know exactly when it will occur, but I do know two things:

1. It's not going to happen now or in the foreseeable future (say, one to four years). You should read *The Great Boom Ahead*, by Harry S. Dent Jr. The author's research (consumer cycles, peaks) points to a current bull market ending around 2007 or 2008. His conclusions are based on baby boomers getting near retirement age. It's a convincing argument. I think if he errs, it is on the short side. Add to his calculations the "boomers" from Russia, China, and India growing older and adding to a worldwide expansion of commercialization, and you'll see why I say that.

2. You can tell the signs of a bear market before they happen. Think about it. If a bear market (however short and insignificant) is caused by certain factors: high interest rates (which could have occurred by a Fed worrying about inflation and which could end with lower corporate earnings occurring simultaneously or close to each other) high taxes, high inflation, and low corporate earnings; and if a bull market is caused by the opposite (low interest rates, relatively low taxes, lower inflation, and good earnings) then the answer is simple: watch for real moves–up or down–in these areas. I say real because the Fed might tinker with rates in response to fears (not actual occurrences) of things that they think are important.

> *It isn't as important to buy as cheap as possible as it is to buy at the right time.*
>
> —JESSE LIVERMORE

The horizon would need to have all three clouds (a storm if you will) coming together. My solution: keep an eye on the horizon but get busy making money. Make hay while the bull climbs.

How? Read on.

2

DOES HISTORY REPEAT ITSELF?

Average earnings of an English worker in 1900 came to half an ounce of gold a week and, in 1979, after world wars, a world slump, and a world inflation, the British worker has an average earnings of half an ounce of gold a week.

—WILLIAM REES MOGG

I t is difficult to keep things in perspective. At the time of the crash of 1987 there were too many comparisons to 1929 to even count. Charts pointed out the likeness of the two events and the likelihood of a repeat performance. Cyclists developed 50-year cycles, 12-year cycles, 4-year cycles, and so on. There were political observers and economists everywhere, each with his or her own theory.

Yes, it is true; there are several similarities between the two events. And yes, there are numerous attempts to make sense or figure out what happened–maybe an attempt to pigeonhole the phenomena, make it understandable, and hence palatable. I reject most of these attempts.

The only thing I agree with is this: a set of circumstances occurs in no particular order. A cause (however minor) starts and a chain reaction commences. The situation, usually totally irrational, takes on a life of its own. The crash (or whatever you want to call it) ends for different reasons and the recovery time period and strengths are totally unrelated.

A strange, but hopefully useful comparison would be Woodstock. I was not there. I was too busy with my own rock-and-roll band. The place, the timing, the participants, the attendees, what preceded the event, the feelings at the event and afterward created "Woodstock." Many attempts have been made to recreate the main event. Thirty years later, one was pulled off that would, in a few ways, parallel the original event. The point being, it was a phenomenon that can't be recreated. It just happened. I'm sure everyone reading this has had such an event. Maybe a honeymoon, a vacation, a special meeting, whatever. Attempts to duplicate it are futile.

> *The worst bankrupt in the world is the person who has lost his enthusiasm.*
>
> —H. W. ARNOLD

So that's what I'd like to accomplish here: give a comparison of the 1929 and 1987 crash, not to prove that they were the same, but to prove that they were not the same. I won't purposefully try to discount any comparisons that match up. I won't have to. You'll see that any likeness usually had different timing and effects.

Why do I make this attempt? Only to educate others so that readers, my seminar attendees, and even my staff will not make decisions based on incomplete or erroneous information. This comparison will be relatively short. It would serve you well to study greater and more comprehensive examinations of this matter. History may not repeat itself exactly, but if we don't study history, we are destined to repeat ourselves.

THE 1929 CRASH

The roaring twenties became a way of life–a feeling. The stock market crash was hardly a crash to Main Street. People were working, factories were humming, and a new religious revival was happening. Speakeasies were around, but were not the norm. The crash took time to permeate everywhere. It took time, but was eventually felt everywhere. It was part of but not the sole reason for the depression that followed.

The buildup to 1929, and even the first half of that year, had progressed at a fairly rapid pace. Many average Americans were buying stocks. Mutual funds were many years in the future, as were derivatives of stocks, like options and other interest rate, index-related securities. But margin investing did exist and was used extensively. The Dow Jones Industrial Average peaked on September 3rd. It turned around, however, and in the first two weeks of October, it rallied to 353.

News happens. On October 15th, the Weekly Production figures came in and US Steel was down 17%. Heavy selling commenced. Back then, the market had a Saturday trading session. US Steel fell $27.75 that week. General Electric and other stocks were down. Obviously, everyone was concerned. A group of big banks got together immediately and committed one billion dollars to bolster the market. This worked, as the market temporarily stopped skidding.

> *The worse a situation becomes, the less it takes to turn it around, the bigger the upside.*
>
> —GEORGE SIROS

On October 24th, one million shares traded in just 30 minutes. Buyers couldn't be found and major companies' stock (even the most previously liquid stock) plunged—sometimes dipping $5 to $10 between trades. That day 12.9 million shares traded. The old one-day record was 8.2 million.

The Wall Street Journal added fuel to the fire. On Monday, October 28th, its headline read, "Stock Market Crisis," and sales orders poured in even before the market opened.

Tuesday, the market fell another 30 points. It closed at 261. It was at 381 on September 3rd, and had fallen 31%. General Motors was at $40 from its high that year of $91.75. General Electric had been $422, now it bottomed at $222.

How could the bad news from US Steel cause a crash? It didn't, but was one log on the fire. No one factor caused the crash. A culmination of events, news, and statements created a selling atmosphere, which eventually created a crash.

CONSIDER

Earnings were okay. They surely didn't seem to be heading lower. Many companies and many experts were looking to a good solid growth pattern extending through 1930. Chrysler shipped 17,000 more cars in 1929 than 1928. Household furnishing orders were up. Typewriter sales were up. Many other companies showed increased earnings on the horizon.

Were stocks expensive? Not in general. Some were, and their high multiples were based on projected future earnings. This is not uncommon. All in all, stocks just didn't seem high priced based on the future. But, on current earnings per share, they were high. For example, General Electric's high of $403 was at price to earnings ratio of 56, or 56 times earnings. See my *Wall Street Money Machine, Volume 1: Revised For The New Millennium,* and *Volume 2: Stock Market Miracles* for more on the importance of price to earnings (P/E) ratios.

When excitement builds and people don't want to get left out, they'll do anything to get in. They'll borrow heavily–home mortgages, personal loans, etc. Margin accounts at brokerage firms were at an all time high. Some allowed investors to put up as little as 10%. Obviously, a downturn would hurt, and this assured extra selling.

No matter how little you've done in life, how much you've abused yourself, whatever your lifestyle, or your occupation, you can improve.

—Nolan Ryan

Think of it. As stocks slid a little, the investor had to cover the collateral by bringing in more stocks or cash. In a full fall they could not cover the margin, and mass selling occurred to stop further erosions. Another log on the fire.

Interest rates were high. Just before September, the Federal Government raised its discount rates from 5 to 6%. This was the fourth rise in rates from 1927. They were raised to stem the flow of gold out of the country. With this negative economic news, foreign investors sold US stocks and bonds before they continued to erode.

Now to another bugaboo, another large log. Congress seemed likely to pass a very restrictive tariff bill, virtually isolating American industries, and restricting their ability to trade freely (or at least less restrictively). Like now, it seems our bungling politicians can't seem to get government out of our pockets, causing more harm than good. *The Wall Street Journal* reported this story on October 28th. It was the Smoot-Hawly Tariff Bill, a bill so damaging in the cause and length of the Great Depression.

If you destroy a free market you create a black market. If you have ten thousand regulations you destroy all respect for the law.

—Winston Churchill

All of these factors together added up to the crash of 1929. No one thing caused it.

The Biggest Crash In History, 1987

The 1987 stock market crash was incredible. The recovery took nowhere near as long as the 1929 crash, but in terms of dollars, its loss was more severe. The market once again turned expensive. Just like

1929, certain specific events led up to the crash. You'll see, except for stock prices being high, no event listed here is the same as 1929.

On October 14th the Dow Jones Industrial average went down 95 points. This set a new record. Why? News came out that the trade deficit for August was $10 billion. This caught people by surprise.

Then the House Ways and Means Committee set about to change the tax filing requirements for mergers between big companies. Such mergers or acquisitions had failed to produce some of the expected price/value increases, and this tax change was seen to have damaging consequences. That Thursday, the Dow Jones Industrial average fell 58 points. The next day, it fell another 108 points. It stood at 2,247: 17% less. A decline from its high on August 25th. Too many logs too fast.

Monday saw a panic. The Dow dropped 508 by the close, going down in major chunks all day long. An astounding number of shares traded that day. I owned stocks at that time, but was so busy running my business, I hardly noticed. When I did, I bought more shares.

Was the 1987 crash like 1929 in its severity? Yes. But in its causes, hardly, except for a few things. Stocks were priced high. In August 1987, for example, the S&P 500 traded at 25 times earnings.

The mass of men lead lives of quiet desperation.
—HENRY DAVID THOREAU

Investors and analysts (brokers) were finding innovative justifications for purchasing stocks at these high prices. One such valuation was modern in nature. Its called "break-up value." Buy a company, even with expensive debt, then sell off divisions or assets, pay off the debt, and pocket the excess. Mergers and acquisitions abounded. Anyone who held onto stocks through the '80s was much better off even after the 30% decline because shareholder value had increased so much.

In 1929, margin usage had been overused. New margin requirements were 50%. However, new forms of "margin" popped up. One was index futures, and options. This allowed investors with small amounts of money to tie up larger positions. The "magnified" movement on these derivatives can make overnight millionaires or overnight paupers.

Another thing occurred in 1985 and 1986. The Federal Reserve (under Paul Volcker) expanded the money supply, up 12% in 1985 and 16% in 1986. This easy money found its way to the stock market. Inflation seemed guaranteed and interest rates were just starting to increase. Stocks seemed like the place to be. Many investors bought into equities.

Mutual fund investing saw billions of dollars pour in from individual investors who "trusted" these big fund managers more than their own instincts. This money had to be invested.

Just like in 1929, the Federal Government's monetary policy shifted two months before the crash. This time it was Alan Greenspan. He replaced Paul Volcker and, on September 3rd, raised the discount rate from 5.5 to 6%.

> *The test of success is not what you do when you are on top. Success is how high you bounce when you hit bottom.*
> —GENERAL GEORGE S. PATTON

The dollar started falling and required foreign investors to finance our debt. The amount of foreign involvement dropped in half. Now, this increase in the interest rates would draw foreign investors back into the game.

After the crash, the Federal Government announced it would provide whatever liquidity the market needed to stem the tide. The market rebounded 150 points by December 31st.

The only really significant comparison is that stocks seemed over-priced. So, this should also be our concern. No single event caused it. Neither wars, impeachments, corporate bankruptcies, nor tragedies of any sort have sent the markets into decline. Crashes are not random events. They occur when a series of negative things happen which affect or infect investor attitudes.

No one knows when, but you will read elsewhere in this book how you can watch the horizon, diversify, stay with some cash, and learn how to play any type of market.

In the realm of ideas, everything depends on enthusiasm, in the real world, all rests on perseverance.
—GOETHE

3

PLAY THE MARKET
AT HAND

I'm a great believer in luck, and I find the harder I work the more I have of it.

—THOMAS JEFFERSON

I teach a simple concept in my real estate seminars: the road to wealth is not a freeway. It has many ups and downs, many detours, and many potholes along the way. The stock market in general, and any single stock in particular, is the same way. You can get a historical chart of any company and you will see a line that looks like the outline of a jagged mountain range, sometimes going up to new highs–the peaks getting higher and the lows become higher as well. Or the complete opposite is true. A stock has three choices: it is either going up, down, or sideways.

As I teach in my live Wall Street Workshops™ and Next Step™ seminars, we need to take advantage of this volatility in stocks. This is the key to the effective use of formulas for generating cash flow. Volatility gives buying opportunities. Volatility is important to qualm fears of a runaway bull market. Whether we're playing the stock or an op-

tion on the stock (either a call option which gives us the right to buy or
a put option which gives us the right to sell) we are going to take
advantage of the turning point of the stock when it reaches a peak or
valley. As one of our WSWS instructors likes to say, "We earn in the
turn." I've covered this extensively in a chapter called Quick Turn Profits in *Wall Street Money Machine, Volume 2: Stock Market Miracles.* I will
not belabor the point here except to say that this is where a lot of
money can be made. We should look at volatility as our friend, not as
our enemy.

Many factors enter into the picture and determine when a stock is
going to bottom out or when it's going to hit its top. Recently there
have been many companies hitting new highs and then, within a month
or two, hit new highs again. There are many plays along the way,
many chances to make money. You can almost bet when a company
hits a new high–especially if it "gaps up" (meaning that it opens up
substantially higher than it closed the day before or unexpectedly rises
or falls intraday outside of its recent pattern–there is a chance to make
money as the stock reverses that "gapped" direction. Then when it hits
its bottom or support level, there is another chance to make money on
the bounce and on the way back up. A stock may test its support several times and when it does so–and as the news starts to change and
the stock starts to move back up–there is still another opportunity to
make money.

> *Money makes money. And the money that money makes
> makes more money.*
> —BENJAMIN FRANKLIN

One of my favorite ways of making money on these dips is to sell
puts on the stock, agreeing to buy the stock at a certain price. I do this
when I want to own the stock. I also do this when I don't want to own
the stock but I just want to pick up the put premium. I agree to take the
stock, but with the hope that the stock is going to rise, the premium
will go down, and I can either buy back the put option at a lower price
or just go ahead and let it expire and keep all the money. I also buy call

options when stocks are low. I can then sell call options when the stock is high. There are many strategies to use and play in regards to the volatility of these stocks.

Now let's move on and talk about the market in general. How do we make ourselves aware of major dips in the marketplace and how do we protect ourselves against them? Here are some thoughts:

1. As I've said in other places in this book, there are telltale signs of when a recession is going to occur. There are also hidden signs of when there's going to be a major market dip. However, most of us will never see these hidden factors because, as small investors, we do not have access to the inside information that the big-time traders have. For example, program traders have a sell order written into the computer for when funds hit a certain level, or for a stock within a fund which hit a certain level (this is true for several funds, including retirement funds and mutual funds). They also have a sell order written that activates when a certain percentage of profit is made. Likewise, when a stock hits a certain price, they place purchase orders for when it goes down.

Luck is the preparation for, recognition of, and proper seizure of opportunity.

—WALTER HEIBY

This type of trading, especially rapid program trading on the sell side, can cause a major dip in the marketplace. After much research on the 1987 crash, I think this was probably the major cause for the crash. Yes, the stocks were running up right before that and there was a nice rapid bull market in the summer and fall of 1987. All this led to a lot of profit taking. Once the selling started, it was almost a panic. Within a day there were millions upon millions of shares being sold by people who wanted to take their profits or who were caught up in the herd mentality. A huge momentum downward in the stock market resulted. Within a day or two the stock market crashed almost

30%. If you think about it, 30% of the value of companies is like letting air out of a tire, it has to hit a support level eventually. It did within a couple of days, and the climb back up started almost immediately. It was a major buying opportunity for a lot of people to take advantage of that serious correction. One result of this is all the changes that were made or imposed by the exchange on program trading after the 1987 crash.

> *Buy a stock the way you would buy a horse. Understand and like it such that you'd be content to own it in the absence of any market.*
>
> —WARREN BUFFETT

2. I believe that corrections, whether they're mini or maxi, are necessary. They shake out a lot of the people who are just in it for the ride and are not serious investors in any particular company. The negativism caused by these changes on corrections stop companies from having hyper-inflated prices. As I mentioned elsewhere, the bears will always be with us and are necessary to keep everything in check. So, we observe the bear market mentality and play it from the opposite side.

3. Diversification is also important. Not only should we have a lot of our money tied up in really good solid investments like blue chip stocks and good group investments like SPY and MDY (see *Wall Street Money Machine, Volume 4: Safety 1st Investing* for more information on these SpiDeRS), we should also be looking to buy stocks that perform well in recessions and when the stock market is going down. These are called "negative beta down" stocks.

There are other measuring sticks which point the way to stocks that perform well in these kind of marketplaces. If you have a high need for safety and security in your stock market investments, you should consider buying these types of stock. If you fear the rapid volatility of a crash, you may want to avoid options. Or, when a stock does start to fall, you may want to buy put options, ride a stock price down, and gain value in your put option as the stock falls. You can also buy call and put options on the overall market, like the SPX, OEX, and DJX. There are many other index options available for sector investing.

4. If you do invest in options in a particular stock you could do short-term plays and long-term plays. I have outlined these in numerous courses and books. You should buy a short-term option at or near the strike price or "slightly in the money" call options. Buy further out options, say four to six months out, and go one or two strike prices above the current stock price just to give yourself some safety (to have a backup hedge on your option plays). However, I do not want to make a six-month out option sound like a panacea remedial action for everything that could happen. If there were a huge 10, 20, or 30% crash in the marketplace, virtually all of your options would be worthless and probably not recover in time. That's why you go back to point number three: you should diversify and not have a lot of your money tied up in riskier option plays.

The word "crises" in Chinese is composed of two characters: the first, the symbol of danger; the second, opportunity.

—ANONYMOUS

Here's an example. Look at July of 1996. I had a small percentage of my portfolio, around $40,000, tied up in several option plays. Now, I had made several hundred thousand dollars, but I lost around $30,000 on July 16th of 1996 when the stock market took a downturn. Look at the timing of this dip. This was not that serious. If you look at the chart for the balance of the year, you can see that the stock market recovered and went way above where it was before the correction. However, on a short-term basis, there was not any way my options could recover–especially the July options–before the expiration date.

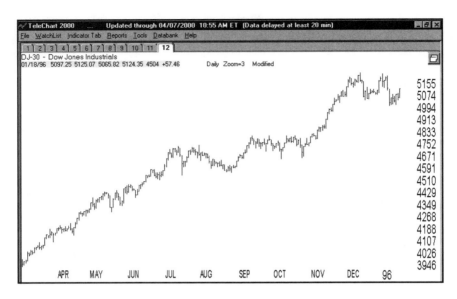

That July dip occurred just a few days before the July expiration date. We were sitting pretty on some of our options on Monday. On Tuesday–the day of the dip–these options went down and became almost worthless. They did not recover by that Friday. So all the options we could have sold on Monday (either breaking even or making a profit) we lost money on, and in just a few days. Nobody knew this was coming. It just happened one day, due to lot of program trading, and sentiment built into the marketplace.

> *Good judgement is usually the result of experience and experience frequently is the result of bad judgement.*
> —ROBERT LOVELL

5.   I've said this repeatedly, but these types of corrections are not only necessary but also good. Many times these corrections occur when the "sky is falling" (people start saying the stock market is too high). They do have their day and they're almost always wrong. In late 1999, the panic cry was the Y2K problem. Once in awhile the market takes a serious dip, but usually the information that causes these corrections is dis-

counted before it ever happens. This is especially true when a major firm is downgrading certain stocks or making comments about the marketplace in general, or we have a comment by Alan Greenspan or another influential person. Wise people and people who've been around for a long time know that ebbs and flows can turn into ebbs and cash flows. That's what I've tried to teach at all my seminars and in my books.

Change favors the informed mind.
                                                    —LOUIS PASTEUR

6. Don't panic. If there is a major correction in the marketplace you will be well served by being very, very patient. Especially with modern day trading as compared to the 1929 crash, which did not cause the recession but preceded the recession of 1932. In today's economy, the stock market arena has huge mutual funds, program trading, and all the technical analysis that has become much more sophisticated than ever before. They are set to defend against sudden, serious dips. Yes, history might repeat itself. Yes, there are certain cycles that may be valid. However, there is no substitute for good solid homework: checking the fundamentals of a company, investing in good solid companies having the highest likelihood for improved earnings, making good returns, earning a lot of money, and increasing their earnings capacity. This is where we should be putting most of our money. If our money is there, a slight correction in the marketplace, or even a serious correction, should not shake us from our underlying premise of value investing. After all, we are investors, not gamblers. We sometimes do quick trades, but the objective is to get more money to invest more solidly.

Now, don't get me wrong. We need to check the storyline of each company and if the storyline has changed–if the company is not profitable anymore–we may want to unload our position and get our money into investments which have the highest likelihood of making money. I have tried to make sure that I am not emotionally involved in any particular company. Yes, I have favorites. Nevertheless, even though I like owning these stocks, I would sell them in a minute if I thought they weren't going anywhere. I like them because they are going places. I learned this in my real estate days. Don't get too involved in a particular property because, when you do, you start making stupid decisions. You should not base your decisions for buying a stock, holding a stock, or selling a stock on any emotional factors at all. It should be done on pure simple mathematics and the best calculation as to how you can make the greatest return possible.

All you need is to look over the earnings forecasts publicly made a year ago to see how much care you need to give those being made for the next year.

—GERALD LOEB

CONCLUSION

The stock market seems to do whatever it takes to make fools out of most people most of the time. In many ways, there's no way to figure out the exact timing of any particular move in the marketplace. What we can do to protect ourselves is to stay diversified, have our money in good investments, and treat aggressive plays for exactly what they are—using only our extra money or money that can be invested and put at risk. Only use, as risk money options money we would not feel too badly about losing.

We need to become not only generalized observers of the marketplace but also specific observers of the stocks we're following. On the road to wealth, we take advantage of the bumps and dips. And, hopefully, enjoy the beautiful scenery along the way.

4

BAD NEWS BEARS

The greatest trouble with most of us is that our demands upon ourselves are so feeble, the call upon the great within us so weak and intermittent that it makes no impression upon the creative energies.

—ORSON SWETT MARDEN

There is a fundamental flaw in the way most people think about success in business or success in their careers. People think there is a major difference between a great company and a not-so-great company or even a bad company. Those of us who have been in business for a long time realize this is just not the case. The major difference between a great company and the next to great or barely great, is often just one or two extra sales, or one extra deal.

Again, if you've had your own business, one or two extra sales a week could make the difference of whether your business makes it or not. If you have large items for sale, one or two extra sales a month could literally determine whether you have the money to make payroll or not. It's that extra little effort, that extra 110 or 120% that some people put out which makes big differences. Having a couple of really great salespeople among all the mediocre people who come and go can make the difference. Having people who truly believe success can be had and strive for it makes all of the difference. It is tough enough to make it in business without negativism entering the picture.

Let's relate this to stock market investing. You have to realize there's going to be negativism.

- A lot of people make their living from being negative. There is a whole cottage industry built up of newsletters and seminars that dwell on or play to people's fears. They try to get people overly concerned with bad things in life. I'm reminded of a story of a lady who was sitting in a seminar about environmental concerns in California. She got really excited and started saying to the speaker, "What, what, what did you say? What did you just say there about the San Andreas Fault? What did you say about earthquakes?" And the speaker said, "Well I said that there is probably going to be a major earthquake in the next billion years." And she says, "Oh, oh, billion years. Shhhheeeewww. I'm really glad you said that because I thought I heard you say a million years." I hope you get the point. A lot of people are worrying about things they should not be worrying about.

> *The facts are unimportant! It's what they are perceived to be that determines the course of events.*
> —R. EARL HADAY

- There are so many people who get petty—tripping over pennies on their way to dollars, thinking negative and small thoughts when such thoughts are not warranted or justified.

- It seems that the daily barrage of media attacks on anything positive has had a major impact on a lot of people's lives. You can hardly open up a newspaper without seeing positive and negative information on viewpoints side by side. I know we have become a nation of naysayers. As long as there are a lot of bad things to read or watch, people will do so. I guess it is true that a news report about good information would not be well read. People are attracted to negative news.

Can you imagine a news report saying something like this: "While all of you were at work today your house went up in value. Yes, the good news is the economy is doing well and your stock portfolio has now increased. You're one step closer to being able to put your child through college." We don't hear things like this. It is always the negative. And the more we hang around the negative and the more our minds are barraged by it, the more of an impact it has on our lives and the more we have to fight to counter it. So what do we do? Let me give you several things that I think will help you make money in the midst of a negative atmosphere.

A statistician is someone who can draw a straight line from an unwarranted assumption to a foregone conclusion.
—ANONYMOUS

1. Consider the source. What is the person disseminating the negative information trying to accomplish? What are they trying to get out of it? More specifically, what are they trying to sell? If it's a newsletter, negativism, no matter how far fetched, sells subscriptions. TV is the same. To keep you watching, they throw in a few fires, accidents, shoot-outs, et cetera. The news reports on the economy and stock market are no different.

2. Why not use this negativity as a barometer to help you decide when to sell different stocks and options? Let me give you a scenario. The stock market does not climb on an even basis. The road is rocky. You would not say that it has even steps like a staircase. Not only are the height and the width of the steps unequal, but the length of them (the overall timing of the steps) is not equal.

As the stock market moves up there are always going to be dips. In *Wall Street Money Machine, Volume 1: Revised For The*

New Millennium I call these "range riders." A stock will start at $20 and go up to $24, but then back off to $22, and then go up to $26, and then back off to $23. Then it will go up to $26½ and back off to $24. It may be two or three weeks or even two or three months between these dips, but as a stock rises, as a company is expanding, as its earnings are growing, a lot of market sentiment enters the picture. It is to this point that I add the following:

The market is only not always right, but it is usually wrong, so why not use this market sentiment to our advantage? People cause change. We are all participants in the marketplace whether we are actually buying stocks or mutual funds, or just shopping at K Mart or Sears. We are participants in the marketplace and, being participants, it is impossible to just sit back and watch. Everything we do affects the price of the stock. Yes, its effects may be small, but there is significance in all of our actions. Taken together, we are the market.

The market is a voting machine, whereon countless individuals register choices which are the product partly of reason and partly of emotion.

—GRAHAM & DODD

Then a lot of market mentality or market sentiment enters the picture. When the stock market rises on good economic news, or the fact that the Chairman of the Federal Reserve is not going to raise interest rates, and the stock market rallies 180 points, you most assuredly know that in the next few days that increase is going to be given back. Maybe not all of it, but quite a bit, say 120 points.

Likewise, when there is either a rumor of bad economic news or actual bad economic news and the stock market takes a dip, it's probably going to get back most of what it lost within the next few days. It's almost as if "what Monday giveth, Tuesday taketh away," and "what Tuesday taketh away, Friday giveth back."

I know it's not exactly that simple, but it almost looks that simple when you examine historical charts. It may not be on a day-to-day basis where it goes up 80 points one day and down 80 points the next day. However, when you see a dip in the marketplace, why not play it as it goes back up?

If you're using the Dow Jones Industrial Average, that's just 30 stocks. Even an uptick or downturn can be from one or two stocks with a lot of trading going on. These stocks are on a weighted basis. It's hard to tell how much impact any one particular stock has on the whole, but if IBM has a serious dip for one day, it is definitely going to take the Dow Jones Industrial Average down. If the Dow Jones Industrial Average goes down 80 or 90 points in one day, why not look into it? Find the two, three, or four stocks that have gone down and buy the stocks or options on the stocks and ride them back up. See, sometimes you can make intraday trades and catch a dip either in a particular stock or in the market as a whole. Sometimes it takes a little longer. Either way, you can make money.

> *In a bull market, an "overbought" condition lasts longer while an "oversold" condition ends very quickly. The reverse is true in bear markets.*
>
> —ALAN R. SHAW

I'm reminded of this continually when I have people coming through our live Wall Street Workshops™. It's almost like a direct challenge is given to me or to our instructors: "Well, the stock market is down 90 points today." They want to see what we'll do. Sometimes, this happens as we get there in the morning at 6:30 A.M Pacific time. The stock market takes a big dip or opens down 40 or 50 points. Some think all hell is breaking loose and the sky is falling once again. Then we turn around and the stock market is down another 40 points, we jump in on a few stocks, and the Dow Jones, within an hour and a half, is up 30 points. Then two hours later, it's down 60 points, and later, it's up 29 points again. Each turn presents an opportunity. These types of trades can be especially profitable if you're playing options. Remember, when there is a small movement in the stock there is a magnified movement in the option. An $80 stock goes to $85 and the $4 (or $4,000) call option goes to $5 (or $5,000) sometimes in hours.

> *Without development there is no profit, without profit, no development.*
> —JOSEPH A. SCHUMPETER

3. If you are going to use options, there are special concerns. Options are very risky, in that they are fixed time investments. When you look at the charts and diagrams of these different plays and strategies you need to make sure that you buy an option far enough out and only when you've studied the movement—the "compelling" reason for it to go up in value. You pick the longest time you possibly can. For example, if a particular stock goes down from $93 to say $85 in one day, then you have to ask, "Why is this stock down? Is the whole market down or is this stock down because of news about other stocks in this same industry?"

    If the stock is down but the whole market is up, that tells you there may be a negative trend and you ought to be calling your stockbroker and asking about the news of the stock. Conversely, if the stock is up and the whole market is down, that could signify very good strength in the company. However, the point is that you're trying to catch the stock at either a recent new high, or a recent bottom (support level). Very seldom does a stock hit a high and then hit a high the next day and the next day and then continue. At some point, usually within a week after its new high, it's going to back off. It may not be down to the point where it was before it ran up to the high, but it's definitely going to back off a little. Now, whether you're going to buy puts on a "peaked out" stock, or buy call options on a dip in the stock, you still need to do them far enough out, at least a full month, but usually two to four months, so that you can weather any vicissitudes in the stock. You get your biggest bang for the buck by buying short-term options, but there is added safety in close-to-the-money options out two to five months.

4. Don't bet all your money on one particular option. Not only should you be diversified in investing smaller amounts of money in many different options on many different stocks, but also within the same stock you should be looking at different strike prices, different expiration months, and most importantly different purchase points. For example, let's say a stock has gone from $93 down to $85 and you go ahead and buy the call option. Let's assume it's June and you buy the August $85 call option for $4 and the stock goes down to $83. Now the $80 call option for August is $4. I hate to use the words "averaging down," but you can buy more at this lower price point. When it takes another dip, you could buy more options at a lower price, or further out options, giving you more time at the same strike price to make money. Then wait for it to come back up from $80 to $85. You may want to buy the October or November options at a higher strike price so that it won't cost so much money. Then, as they increase in value, sell all or part and take your profits.

> *Quality is never an accident; it is always the result of high intention, genuine effort, intelligent direction, and skillful execution.*
>
> —Willa A. Foster

The point is that there are many different plays and many times to get involved. At no point in time should you be investing all of your money into one option, one strike price and one month on one particular company. Diversification is the key.

Let's use negative, even intraday, comments as a way to watch trends. I'm saying we should not be too involved in the particular movements of the stock unless we are really trying to play a quick turn. I have a whole section on that type of transaction in *Wall Street Money Machine, Volume 2: Stock Market Miracles.*

> *Unless you've interpreted changes before they've occurred you'll be decimated trying to follow them.*
> —ROBERT J. NUROCK

We could also look at the market as a whole—catching the trend of the entire marketplace. If you look at the market as a whole over the past _____ years (you fill in the blank, it won't matter how many you choose), you'll notice there's been an upward trend. The average compounded returns over the years have been about 16%. I know my students who have attended the Wall Street Workshop™ are doing far superior to that, sometimes getting 16% in a week or two (not annual returns).

Let's go back to intraday trades and see if we can look at the comments that happen either on a weekly or monthly basis, comments from newspapers and newsletters. If you hear many people saying that the market is either going to crash or the stock prices are too high, then look at the particular stocks you are following and see if what they're saying is relevant.

For example, imagine you have a stock that you bought around $70 and it has slowly climbed up to $77. Now, on merger information or good news about its earnings, the stock pops up to $92. At $92 everybody is saying that not only is the market going to crash but that this stock is way overpriced. Just the fact that a lot of people are talking negative about this company will have a very dramatic and negative impact, and usually a very quick impact, on the company's stock. This could get even more pronounced if several of the major brokerage houses are recommending this stock as a strong buy, and all of the sudden change their recommendation.

Rationalize this one through with me: brokers still like the stock but they liked it better when it was at $70. Now that it's at $92 they need to look at it once again. The stock has gone from a strong buy to a buy or to a hold recommendation. The stock has risen to a point where they will not recommend to their clients that they should buy it. If that is the case, a lot of people will perceive (and that's all it is—a perception, usually by naive people) that this company's stock may not be good anymore. You'll see a whole lot of selling going on. At least it will stop the run-up.

You may do better to go ahead and sell your stock at $92 and pick it up again at $82 or $85 after the shakeout occurs. This is basically trying to stay ahead of the herd. If you can't get ahead of the herd, follow the herd only to a certain extent. Yes, yes, yes, yes, there may be many momentum investors, but when the stock hits $92 they start jumping in because they see all the activity. You may want to look again at the Balance of Power™ (a proprietary indicator in TeleChart 2000® by Warden Brothers) in the stock, the difference between the volume of buying and selling.

> *Buy on the rumor, sell on the news.*
>
> —MARKET MAXIM

Many charting services give this information. Try to find out about the cash going into the stock as compared to the cash going out of the stock. Basically, it's the number of buyers and the numbers of shares being sold as compared to the number of shares being purchased and at what prices. So the Balance of Power™ (how much buying and selling is going on) can be a good indication whether $92 is a top. You may want to hang around just a little bit more and ride it from $92 to $94, but at some point in time, all the negative information is going to play out and become real. Instead of just a report about the stock, it will become actual selling.

I think at this point in time you would have rather sold the stock at $92 than to have had it run up, even within an hour or the next day, to $94, then back off to $88 before the day is over. Again, don't get greedy.

Realize that on any particular run up in the stock there will be many people who will come out of the woodwork and start bad-mouthing the company. More particularly, they will start bad mouthing the price range that the stock is currently in. Even though the company may be well run and solid fundamentally, the negative talk may drive down the price of the stock, again usually temporarily.

> *Successful investing is anticipating the anticipations of others.*
>
> —JOHN MAYNARD KEYNES

To wrap this section up, we want to take any of the bad market sentiments and use them to our advantage. We don't want to be an ostrich with our head in the sand, but we also don't want to overreact to negative news and pull ourselves completely out of the marketplace.

We should use negative talk to time our entry into the marketplace on any particular stock: to choose a very, very wise and good time to get involved. My feeling is this: while the true bears are not only always going to be with us in the same numbers as of late, there will always be negative people who are overly vocal—no matter what happens. Also, there are always people who look at the same market statistics and numbers and the same economic factors, but interpret them a different way.

From my experience, there are negative people and they do have a negative impact. The fact that they are always there does not mean that what they say is true. As a matter of fact, it's almost impossible to find a "bear-sayer" who has been right two quarters in a row. In the last five to eight years, they have been so badly off target that they hardly have any credibility. It is at this point in time that we want to be careful. With the market rising, the bears may have a tendency to shut up, but we want them there. They cause movement and volatility and keep us from complacency.

We want them saying their negative things. If you follow the Wade Cook stock market strategies, we thrive on volatility; we profit from quick turns, bottoms, peaks, and other "newsy" moves. Whether the strategy is range riders, rolling stocks, or reverse range riders for our stock plays, or quick turn option plays, we need a lot of buying enthusiasm going on when stocks take a dip; we also need a lot of selling enthusiasm going on when stocks rise to unprecedented heights. I'm into "irrational exuberance."

> *Don't compete, create. Find out what everyone else is doing and then don't do it.*
>
> —JOHN WELDON

What you're going to do with this depends on where you are personally. Are you positive or negative? Do you play the positive side of the market or the negative side? I contend that you should not gamble on pessimism. You should also not throw all your eggs in the basket of optimism, but if you're going to err, err on the side of the stock market going up, of companies continuing to thrive, of companies continuing to expand overseas, and of companies trying to bring more value to their shareholders. Err on the positive side, and you'll err less often.

5

INCOME STRATEGIES

Knowledge born from actual experience is the answer to why one profits; lack of it is the reason one loses.

—GERALD LOEB

B uying and selling options to purchase stock are simple strategies loaded with opportunities regardless of the market's direction. The inherent risk of options is that they expire, or go down substantially in price and never recover before the expiration date. However, they can generate fantastic returns in a relatively short amount of time. This is because option prices move up and down in correlation with the price of the stock, but on an exaggerated basis depending on the time until expiration. If you haven't already read my books on stock market strategies, I suggest you do so soon. *Wall Street Money Machine, Volume 2: Stock Market Miracles*, and *Volume 4: Safety 1st Investing* are loaded with detailed, step-by-step outlines of each strategy that I have tried and tested myself to ensure maximum returns with minimum risk.

Following is a very brief synopsis of some of those strategies. Remember, when you buy or sell an option, you buy or sell the right, not necessarily the obligation, to exercise the underlying stock.

These ways of making money have several things in common.

1. They are definitely about generating cash flow—actual money hitting the account.

2. They generate cash quickly—usually in two to six weeks.

3. They lend themselves to duplication. My motto is: "Don't do anything which can't be duplicated," sung to the tune of "I'd rather lose money and know how I lost it, than make money and not know how I made it." But I'll never lose money for long.

4. They are easy to understand—I love teaching strategies and plays that I, a former cab driver, and most of my students are able to do.

5. The downside risk is mitigated: the risk is lessened either by the inherent nature of the strategy, or by all the cautions I've built into the particular way I use the formulas.

6. Some can be done in a "tax free environment." This is difficult for many people to understand. Some people have heard of tax free investments, like a municipal bond, but most have not heard of a tax free entity which makes all forms of investing tax free (Keogh Plans, IRAs, SEP IRAs, 401(k)s and the best, a Corporate Pension Plan).

7. The strategies and formulas almost become self-perpetuating. The added cash profits can be used for safer and more blue chip style investing, or add to the cash for their trades.

My staff and I teach 13 different cash flow strategies at the Wall Street Workshop™. Most of these are covered in my books–not with the same vivacity of actually doing deals, but at least covered. A very brief glance at a few of the 13 strategies are listed here. Variations of these plays will help build cash flow, purchase additional growth or cash flow assets, and mitigate any damage done by a bear market, or a brief downturn.

WADE'S STRATEGIES

BOTTOM FISHING

This is a simple way of finding stocks that are severely underpriced, or at least ones that you think have a high likelihood for going much higher.

Stocks in this category could come from:

- Really bad news.
- Bankrupt (Chapter 11) companies on their way out of bankruptcy.
- Turnarounds, mergers, and spin-offs.
- Companies just going public or just getting listed on an exchange.
- Companies breaking out of their roll range with better earnings, new products, et cetera.
- Traditional penny stocks with some reason (pressure) for the stock to go up.

BOTTOM FISHING IN A BEAR MARKET

We want to buy stocks in a metaphorical pressure cooker–having all the characteristics of a pot ready to explode. In a bear market these turnarounds, coming out of bankruptcy, new start ups, et cetera, probably won't explode, but if the proper homework is done, if you get in early and stay diversified, then the ride should be profitable.

This may also be a good time to review the stocks you already own: say Bottom Fishing stocks you purchased previously–in this past bull market. Do they have strength? Are they widely held, or not? Would a recession take the wind out of their sails? Or, are they strong, with new and better earnings? Are they up in a down market? In short, are they still a keeper? In a good market, use these to build income and use that income to buy quality stocks.

BUY GOOD COMPANIES

This strategy is just what it says. Good, well-organized, well-managed companies with good products are good investments in any market. See *Wall Street Money Machine, Volume 4: Safety 1st Investing* for much more on building a great blue chip portfolio or attend the Wall Street Workshop™. Remember prices change quickly, value changes slowly. We look for value, and then buy at a good price.

CALL OPTIONS

A call option is the right to buy a specific stock. You buy call options when you think the stock is going up. This could be after a slam (serious down movement), on a roll (when the stock is at the bottom of a roll range), or when a stock has good news, et cetera. In short, when you think the stock has pressure to move up, buy a call, ride it up, and sell. Since many stocks go down when the whole market dips, call options can be bought and sold quickly. Outright purchasing calls can be hazardous in a down trending market. Buy puts or do bear call spreads.

DUCKS

Some of you have read elsewhere about DUCks–or Dipping Undervalued Calls. Usually

CALL OPTIONS IN A BEAR MARKET

Avoid call options on companies that have peaked. Watch earnings carefully. Look for serious slams ($10 to $13 dips) and be patient–wait for clear signs of strength. Read the "Dead Cat Bounce" section in *Wall Street Money Machine, Volume 2: Stock Market Miracles.*

Don't always go for doubles, take 20 to 40% quick returns and look for other quick movers. DON'T try to catch a falling piano.

DUCKS IN A BEAR MARKET

In buying stocks, buying calls, or selling puts; we want the balance of buying power to be occurring after a stock split, this is when a stock that has been climbing pulls back temporarily as investors take their profits. The company is solid and growing, but the stock dips 5 to 10% for no reason other than profit taking. Around our office, we have a word for this. We call it a "SALE." The price of the stock and also of the options has just dropped below its time value. It is a perfect buying opportunity.

HEDGING

One use for options is to "hedge." A hedge is like an insurance policy. You hedge to limit your downside. Let's say you just spent $10,000 and purchased 100 shares of stock at $100 each. You think the stock is low (either the company is really profitable or that the stock has gone down and hit a new low). $10,000–that's a lot of money to have tied up. You have unlimited upside potential and all the time in the world because you actually own the stock. Your risk is a dip in the price of the stock.

However, this can be a considerable risk. So, you hedge. You have two choices:

• You sell a put option at a strike price near the price you spent on the stock. This way

positive. In a down market we sell on peaks, quick run ups, and on major bad news. Not every stock recovers right away. In a down market it may take months (instead of weeks) for a stock to become a buy once again.

you gain the premium as insurance if the stock price goes
down and stays down.

• You buy the short-term puts
at a comfortable strike price
out three to six months and
then reevaluate the situation
as they expire. If the stock
goes down the value of your
put option increase, compen-
sating for a price dip in the
stock.

You also use this strategy if
you have stocks that have sig-
nificantly increased in value and
you want to protect your upside
gains.

*This is to let you know that during the five business days
following the Wade Cook Wall Street Workshop™, I averaged
approximately $250 a day using only the covered calls
technique I learned during the workshop. In addition, by
working with a full-service broker, I was able to obtain 500
shares of a strong "takeover" stock for a possible 30 to 40%
profit. All things considered, I am confident I have started on
a realistic course to financial independence. Thanks to all in
Seattle for their time and expertise. Wade was correct when
he said the workshop is worth more than 10 times the tuition
amount.*

—RICHARD S., WA

PEAKS AND SLAMS

Every day there are several
stocks that close several dollars
higher. They usually move
higher on news. Sometimes, but
very seldom, they do so for no
reason whatsoever. The good

PEAKS AND SLAMS IN A BEAR MARKET

A down market will look like
a reverse range rider. We've used
reverse range riders for years so
the strategy is the same. Buy on
lows and sell on highs. Even if

news is usually about earnings—and if the earnings are great, the new high might be sustained, but if it's something other than earnings, i.e. a takeover, a merger, new product, stock split, et cetera, the good news can play out very quickly.

As in the "Dead Cat Bounce" strategy, the peak strategy happens very quickly. You have to be ready to move not only on the purchase but also on the sell. I usually know my exit (sell price) when I get involved. I believe we live in a very short-term society. We forget good news in about three days. It takes three months to forget bad news. This is only my conjecture, "the gospel according to Wade." I have no empirical evidence to back up the three-day/three month statement, only a string of profitable trades using this as a guideline.

ROLLING OPTIONS

Options allow you to invest in the big stocks by proxy, using a small amount of money. Buy calls or sell puts when a stock is in its low range and then buy puts, or sell calls when it peaks out and starts back down. This gives you a way to make money on both sides of the movement. This is "two plays up and two

you're a little off the mark, you should still be profitable. Be careful, and check the charts. Find a broker who is good at technical analysis to help you enter and exit in a more effective manner.

ROLLING OPTIONS IN A BEAR MARKET

This is one of the best "predictable" cash machines. Get good at looking at charts. Check the momentum indicators (from your charting service or from your broker). Options are risky, so be careful. Make sure the stock, and hence the option, is heading in the desired direction.

plays down." You can add more swing or roll plays with spreads.

In a down market, consider buying a little more time–say out three to four months, instead of one to two months. Use rolling options in good and bad times.

ROLLING STOCK

There are certain stocks that trade within a certain range. Some brokers call this channeling. These stocks move up to a high (resistance) and then down to a low (support). Many stocks do this, but the ones I like (so I don't have a lot of cash tied up) are cheaper stocks–say in the $1 to $5 range. I find a stock that goes from $2 to $2.75. It doesn't seem like a lot of profit, but 75¢ on a $2 investment in one to four months is not bad.

The three rules of rolling stocks are:

- You always know your exit before you go in the entrance.
- Don't get greedy–sell below the high for quick and sure profits.
- Stick with the less expensive stocks so you can buy more.

SPREADS

Spreads, as in bull put spreads and bear call spreads (my two favorites) let us play the swing movements. Spreads help you limit exposure to large risks. They help reduce margin

ROLLING STOCK IN A BEAR MARKET

This strategy still creates predictable returns. Believe it or not, many stocks roll faster in down (or flat) markets. More people are watching the news. News makes stocks roll. Stick to the rules in both types of markets.

SPREADS IN A BEAR MARKET

Consider bear call and bear put spreads. Also, practice trades and learn more about puts. In a downtrending market you can make money faster with puts then with calls. The good news requirements. Spread's risk and profit can be pre-calculated.

plays are faster and the bad news hangs around longer.

> *Wade Cook's workshop…was a skeptical seminar for me to go to, even though I have invested in the stock market for several years. My first attempt at options was at the WSWS last week. I generated $3,256 in one day while at the workshop! Since then, in the next week, I made another $2,270. I am excited about the opportunity to be home with my children while I am making money for my husband's and my retirement. Thank you for teaching me a few formulas and giving me a hands-on experience.*
>
> —DAWN, CA

SELLING PUTS

Obviously, any buy opportunity on a rising stock also presents a great opportunity to sell a put and generate income. If the stock turns and rises, you keep the premium and that's it. Of course, you want to pick the stock near the bottom of the dip and sell the put for the very next month out expiration date. The strike price should be very near or just below the stock price. You want protection.

If you're wrong and the stock gets put to you (you may be required to buy it), you get it at a wholesale price. When you buy a stock, you can sell later for a profit, sell covered calls, or just hold it. DUCks and selling puts

SELLING PUTS IN A BEAR MARKET

Selling puts is my favorite cash flow strategy. It's a cash flow generator and if you actually take the stock, you do so at wholesale prices.

This is one strategy you should get good at. Watch the margin requirements. If you get put the stock, sell covered calls, and on the next rebound sell the stock. Don't wait too long. This formula is used to produce income. In down markets you should probably buy back the option (unwind the deal) and roll out. Remember we don't sell puts to buy the stock, but to generate income. Know your exit points!

really present a great opportunity to enhance your cash flow.

SHORT SELLING

Short selling allows you to borrow stock, sell it, and generate income. As the stock moves down, you purchase it, pay off the loan (borrowed stock) and pocket the difference. It's easier said than done.

SHORT SELLING IN A BEAR MARKET

In any down market the "shorts" come out of the woodwork. They are hoping for a continued down elevator. Consider the following:

- You can check the short sales on a particular stock. Your choice then is to join in the crowd (I don't) or wait it out and catch it on a bounce (I do).
- Sometimes heavy short selling becomes a self-fulfilling prophecy. Be careful.
- Put option volume is also a good indicator of a downturn in a stock or in the whole market.
- The bears on a particular stock can kill you, wait and beware.

I've never been big into short selling. There are just to many other wonderful and optimistic ways to make money in the market.

STOCK SPLITS

One of my favorite strategies is to buy call options on companies doing a stock split. We get the best of both worlds, which synergistically really heats up the cash flow. There are many reasons why companies

STOCK SPLITS IN A BEAR MARKET

Announcements of stock splits are seriously curtailed in bear markets. Think of it. Most companies announce splits when their stocks are high—after several quarters or even years of good earnings. But they may announce a stock split, or a stock dividend.

There is a tendency, once a company does a stock split, for the stock to regain "lost ground" over a period of time. (Our experience has shown however, that more times than not, stocks usually go through a short-lived sell-off period immediately after the split.) It may take a year or two or more, but think of that: If a $100 stock becomes two shares at $50, and one to two years later it is flirting with $100 again, you would double your money. What if, as a play, you purchased ten such stocks? One doesn't go anywhere; seven double in a year or so; one doubles in six months; and one doubles in a year and the stock splits again. Wow!

TANDEM PLAYS

There are many combinations, but my favorite is a combination of buying and selling calls and buying and selling puts. Here is how it works (See the chapter "Tandem Plays" in *Wall Street Money Machine, Volume 2: Stock Market Miracles* for more on this.):

When the stock is low, sell a put and buy a call—both strategies gain advantage with an increase in the stock price. You

make an announcement to bolster the price of the stock in a bear market. If so, check earnings, debt, and growth projections. Make sure it's not just a PR play.

My formula is to play options on stock splits. In a down market, the announcement or actual split may be the news needed to get a quick bump out of the stock or option. Don't put too much money into options as they are too risky.

TANDEM PLAYS IN A BEAR MARKET

In a bull market you maximize your cash flow returns. You use formulas in tandem with each other. Use these "combo" strategies to load up. Then in a downturn, use these formulas sparingly and wisely.

Build up your "cash flow" asset base now. Make hay while the bull runs.

make money now selling the put and you make more money later selling the call option you previously purchased. When the stock is high, sell the call and buy a put, or buy back the put you previously sold. You make money on each play as the stock moves down. By using options you have four plays on a rolling stock.

UNCOVERED CALLS

This is called "going naked," in that you don't own the stock. You use this strategy when the stock is at the high part of its range. You sell the call–generating pure cash. You wait. As the stock moves down, your obligation to deliver (sell) the stock goes down and eventually disappears as the option expires. You make money with no investment. The risk is that if the stock goes up, you'll have to buy it at a higher price (offset by the cash you made for selling the call). You can place a buy stop on the stock so you won't lose if the stock moves high. You only do this when the stock has peaked or for some other reason is going down.

UNCOVERED CALLS IN A BEAR MARKET

Think of this: If the stock is going down, selling calls on a stock and not having to deliver the stock is a pure cash generator. Make sure you sell the calls when the stock is on a run up or new high.

This strategy lets you stay a little greedy. BUT don't sell naked calls on stocks that you think are going up. Either buy the stock low and wait to sell the call–getting a higher premium for the options and then eventually sell (get called out) the stock at a higher price, or sell the call when the stock is high–wait for a dip and then:

- buy the stock so you are covered, or
- buy back the option at a lower price (pocketing the profit), or
- just let the option expire and keep the cash!

WRITING COVERED CALLS

Covered calls allow you to get consistently solid monthly returns of 14 to 24%. The idea behind this strategy is that you own the underlying stock and don't mind keeping it. However, the stock price is fluctuating. So, you sell (write) a call option on your stock for whatever price you can get. Your position is "covered" because you own the stock. Even if you sell the stock (and get called out), you can buy it back at a lower price and repeat the strategy or just hold the stock. If you don't get called out you can generate more income next month by selling call options once again.

WRITING COVERED CALLS IN A BEAR MARKET

This is a good way to generate extra income on stocks you already own. If your stocks are down in price then sell slightly out of the money calls, so you'll more than likely not get called out. You keep the stock. Several months of incoming call premiums may be just the trick you need to make back any losses in a down turn in the stock.

You will probably get called out of less stocks (actually sell) in a down market

That's about it. I hope you see the possibilities in a bear market. Yes, it's easier to make money in a bull market, but the preceding strategies are real ways to cash flow the market when its down or going down

6

AN INTERVIEW

Keep away from people who try to belittle your ambitions. Small people always do that, but the really great make you feel that you, too, can become great.

—MARK TWAIN

Very, very rarely, do I have an opportunity to get together with Team Wall Street–a group of the speakers who have taught the Wade Cook Wall Street Workshop™, and people from my Research and Trading Department. To get everyone together at one time in Seattle to record interviews in a studio is really a thrill. The following are excerpts from a discussion we recently held with them. I thought we'd do the interview as a free-for-all, so you can feel their passion, their divergent points of view, and their insights.

WADE: Hi, this is Wade Cook. I'm here today to alleviate some fears that seem to occur whenever we have a robust market and the bears come out of the woodwork. People start talking negatively and thinking negatively. I'd like you to join with me in discussing some of the things that we can do to watch out for, to avoid, to prepare for, and to profit from, any downturn in the current market. And I welcome all of you here. It's good to have you here because it's an opportunity for everybody to get together and discuss the market. You're all traveling and you meet all sorts of people and hear all sorts of ideas on the market. Because of that, you have many diverse viewpoints. I want to hear and discuss those, so, let's talk about a bear market. Where is all this talk coming from?

KEVEN: Well, I think you made the point already that whenever we have such a robust market as we've had for the last several years, everybody always wants to focus on when it's going to end and how bad things are going to get.

JOEL: Whenever you have something good going on you're going to have somebody out there naysaying it.

WADE: So they are bad-mouthing it? For what purpose?

KEVEN: Well, most of the investors have followed conventional wisdom, which says that we need to buy stock and hold it. That's where the money is made. And if there is no effort made to take the profit when it's there when the stock is high, then move out and wait for the best point to jump back in. Those kinds of people will naturally fall prey to the market.

WADE: Okay, let's define a bear market before we go on. Let's ask somebody from our trading department. Pete, will you define what a bear market is?

PETE: Well, a bear market is anything from nine months to two years of a downturn in the market.

WADE: How much? What percentage of a downturn?

PETE: You can expect to see a 20 to 30% drop in the total equities in the DOW, or even in the Standard and Poors 500, or in the NASDAQ.

WADE: What if the market turns down in even a one or two month period of time? For example, the DOW goes from where it was in the summer of 98 at 9,400, then drips to 7,500, and now it's over 10,000.

JOEL: The market is always fluctuating, you're always going to have those little ups, those little downs, you're going to have a month when it slides off a few points. That doesn't mean it's a bear market. The downward trend has to be sustained.

WADE: You say you always have up and downs. Do you think that they are necessary?

JOEL: Well, since the market's emotional more that it is statistical, people tend to say, "Well, I've got my money, let's move out now," or, "Gee, I'm scared right now." You know, they have 1,000 emotions out there, so the market moves in bumps instead of moving smoothly.

RICH: I feel that's a valid point. Also, it works in the way of checks and balances on the system. The soft spots make people evaluate stocks and the market as a whole.

WADE: You're saying then that it's healthy for the marketplace to have a few soft spots?

RICH: I certainly believe it is. If you get into the situation where you just have a true bull market, usually you're going to have the things that are going to be associated with that. Usually the rest of the economy is doing quite well. But, as that economy does well, as wages go up, you're going to have inflation going up, and there will be a tendency to have a runaway economy. You need to have these checks and balance systems in place, just to soften the market up every now and then to keep things in a good perspective.

JOEL: You know, whether it's good for the market or not, it's good for me.

RICH: Definitely, there are moneymaking opportunities there.

WADE: What causes a bear market? Not a crash, we can talk about crashes too, and a crash is obviously associated with a bear market, to a certain degree. But what causes a bear market?

RICH: There can be a number of factors. The main ones are bad corporate earnings and higher inflation.

WADE: How are bad earnings, higher inflation, and other factors tied together?

JOEL: The market pulls back because people pull their money out of it. And they take their money out of it because they're afraid. When you have high inflation, high interest rates, low earnings, people are afraid they're not going to continue to make money–that their stocks will not continue to go up. If it pulls back, it becomes a self-fulfilling prophecy.

WADE: Those are the three causes of a bear market: low earnings, high interest rates, and high inflation.

KEVEN: For at least the first downturn. From there it becomes protracted if the economy really does go south with the market or they interplay together. From that point, you have people who are making less money combined with the fear factor of this big dip in the market. You have a reluctance to come back in with fresh money.

WADE: So you're saying that people may have gotten burned and it becomes tough for them to get back in.

JOEL: Yeah. And people start looking for safer investments–CDs, bonds, et cetera–which higher inflation makes more attractive.

WADE: We don't need to belabor this point. Basically, in America, a bear market is caused by low corporate earnings, which are tied to or stem from high interest rates, or the fear that there's going to be high interest rates.

JOEL: And trade barriers and taxation. Those are two more factors.

WADE: Taxation?

JOEL: Absolutely. A company that is spending much of its profits on taxes isn't going to grow because they have little money to re-invest.

WADE: And if there are high individual taxes, people have less money to spend. All right, so what about trade barriers? We've got NAFTA, GATT; do these have any effect?

JOEL: We've got so much of the world's population now that is interested in advancing their lifestyle and so forth, and the companies that are going to help them do that, many of them are located right here. So as companies expand internationally and continue to grow in phenomenal ways, like Coke and Caterpillar and Pepsi and McDonald's, the results will be phenomenal. We were thinking clear back in 1981 that McDonalds was topped out. Since then it's quintupled or five times its value as they move internationally, it's unreal.

WADE: I've decided that one good way of playing the international marketplace is to buy stock in American companies that are expanding overseas.

RICH: As long as the world economy is doing well, a lot of these companies are getting a significant portion of their profits from overseas.

JOEL: Right. All you have to do is do a little better homework, make sure that you're investing in the companies that are in the expanding markets.

WADE: I think that the rest of the world needs and/or wants so much of what we have. Especially when it comes to our biotech, our pharmaceuticals, our hi-tech computer hardware, software, et cetera.

There are three bull markets for every bear market. And by the way, just a quick note for anybody out there listening, if we've defined a bear market as a market that is down because of low corporate earnings, high taxes, high inflation rates, or high interest rates, then obviously the other side of that coin is that a bull market means good corporate earnings, relatively low taxes, relatively low inflation rates, and relatively low interest rates. So, that's the difference between the bear market and a bull market. In one you have rising stock prices, in the other you have falling stock prices. So my question is, do you see a bear market?

JOEL: The reason why there are such widespread bear market predictions, I think, is the market has always had this general uptrend, the broad 100, 200-year average of this general uptrend. And then we saw in 1995 and right in the beginning of 1996, a sudden escalation of that. The market wasn't just going up gently, it suddenly screamed like a jet aircraft taking off. And so, when it slowed down in 1996, into 1997, and again in 1998 back to the gradual, but rapid climb that it had done earlier and you know, all the way back up, people said, "Oh, no, it's topped out. It's going to fall." Well, what makes them think so?

WADE: Well, because they think the corporations, I guess, can't keep earning money. They can't keep expanding, they can't keep growing.

JOEL: So they have no faith in the American system at all?

WADE: There's so much negativism out there and I get it everywhere I go. It's almost as if before I can teach people to make money, I have to deal with three or four negative people that show up just to be negative.

RICH: One thing I was going to say about the negativism on the economy is that it has a snowball effect because if enough people start saying that the economy is going to go bad, it almost eventually will, just because of all the negativism that comes in with that.

WADE: It becomes a self-fulfilling prophecy.

RICH: Exactly, a self-fulfilling prophecy, just like a snowball that keeps rolling down the hill, it just keeps getting bigger and bigger, just keeps rolling faster. And even though the indicators may not be there, we could go into the bear market. Fortunately, if the other indicators are still pretty positive, it's going to be a very short-lived one.

KEVEN: The question is, where is the world going to go? Are we going to go that direction? Or are those third world countries going to come in this direction?

WADE: They need what we have.

PETE: And look at democracy growing in the world. They obviously want what we have.

WADE: Let's get specific now. What do investors need to do now to get ready for or to avoid a bear market? Yes, at some time we are going to have a downturn, or a major dip in the marketplace, a 20 to 30% dip. Whether it recovers in six months or a year and a half, sometimes the answer is so what? Let me just tell you what I'm thinking, and then you can comment. The negative talk usually doesn't make people money. All it does is use fear to keep investors from entering the market. I'm so tired of that stodgy old thinking. So, what do people do to get ready for a bear market?

KEVEN: The first comment I would make, Wade, is that you hit it right on the head. People talk about investing as they have practiced it for the last 80 or 100 years, it's all buy and hold. You buy a stock and you wait.

WADE: And you can't control what happens then.

KEVEN: There's no money in it. You are like a little tiny ship, tied to a big ship. And wherever the big ship goes, you go with it, whether you want to or not.

WADE: Right. So what are you saying? To not do that?

KEVEN: No, there's a time and a place for that, but it's certainly not a way to make money or get rich. You're going to ride over every wave, you're going to take every downturn along with the market instead of getting more profitable and waiting for another opportunity to use formulas to make money.

WADE: That's a good point.

JOEL: That philosophy, the buy and hold, is actually what you should be doing at the end of a bear market. That's where that plays in. People who have that mentality are thinking we're always at the end of a bear market. I was thinking that there are three things that we can do to deal with a bear market.

1. We need to play the market at hand. You can't go through life trying to play something that doesn't exist.

2. We need education. We need to know what to do, when and if. We need to become familiar with all of the different kinds of markets, the different kinds of stocks, different kinds of plays, and the different strategies.

3. We need a cash reserve. If we, in fact, do go into a bear market, then that cash we are holding is going to enable us to buy some really top-quality companies while they are on "sale."

RICH: But Joel brought up the underlying philosophy to this whole thing, you need to have the knowledge. To have that knowledge, to get the education, to have this know-how to be able to deal with these types of factors in the market. This is the essence.

WADE: To know when to get in?

RICH: To know when to get in and more importantly, know when to get out. The emphasis is on selling.

WADE: All right, you said three, I'm going to add number four. Diversify. I don't want to have anybody coming to my seminars who do not learn the underlying principle of diversification. It's the "not having all your eggs in one basket." So, for example, you might have $10,000 but don't put $10,000 into one stock. Or one option. Put $10,000 into ten different stocks at $1,000 each, right? Take a gamble on ten of them, instead of one. Buy ten good stocks. All right, but I want to spend just a second and not talk about diversification of stocks. What about diversification of formulas? Diversification of methods or ways of making money?

JOEL: Absolutely, it's critical. People think of diversification and they think that means to buy different stocks, so they do. I mean, we have to diversify by sector, by companies, by strategies, by methods, by everything.

WADE: Okay, let's just go through a quick list here. And let's isolate any of these strategies that are pre-bear market in nature. And when I say pre-bear market, I mean getting ready for a bear market, trying to build up and make as much cash as you possibly can. So when there is a downturn of 10, 20, or 30%, your $10,000 has grown to $200,000 before that. A 20% dip takes you down to $160,000. While everybody else is boo-hooing the market with their $10,000 saying, "See, I sat this one out, I didn't get caught in the bear market, we're still sitting pretty." Anybody listening right now could have their $10,000, or be sitting with $160,000. The $160,000 may be partially in cash to allow more buying opportunities. A 20% downturn doesn't look so bad.

Now, how do they build up to $200,000?

Rolling Stock. When a stock rolls between a certain range, it rolls up and rolls down repeatedly, it is a rolling stock.

Writing Covered Calls. Buying stock and selling options on it to generate income, and hopefully getting some capital gains along the way. It is a way of generating income so they have more profits to buy more stock.

Bottom Fishing. Finding IPO's, turnarounds, companies that are coming out of bankruptcy, and other companies that have the highest likelihood of bouncing back or going back up very quickly.

Selling Puts. You agree to buy stock at a certain price and you get paid for that agreement. You literally put yourself out there saying, "I'm willing to buy this stock at this price," and you're hoping the stock goes up and you may not have to buy it, but even if you do, you get paid for the obligation that you took on that play.

Stock Splits. Pure investing in companies that are doing stock splits, by buying the stocks, or by buying options.

PETE: That's really easy, because these formulas put you in a short-term cash flow strategy. You can be in and you can be out of the market before the bear hits.

WADE: So you're saying that a lot of people need short-term strategies?

PETE: Oh, absolutely. I mean, even in a bull market you need a short-term strategy.

WADE: But what you have been saying all along is opposite from what everybody else is teaching. What every stockbroker, every analyst, every company on Wall Street is doing is buy and hold.

PETE: Well not everyone. There's Wade Cook.

WADE: But, I'm serious, I feel so sorry for people. All they do is call their stockbrokers and it's buy this stock and hold on. And they never hear, "Hey, buy the stock at $3 and when it gets to $5, sell it. Then buy again at $3 and sell again for a profit." They don't hear that.

RICH: And they are leaving so much money on the table that way.

JOEL: There are some brokers who are teaching these methods. It's just not very many. The folks who are teaching it do it for a couple three years, then they are wealthy enough to retire in Tahiti, and then who's teaching it?

WADE: Right.

KEVEN: I heard a really interesting comment last week in an Anaheim workshop. This gentleman approached us and said, "I have a friend who is in a major brokerage in San Francisco and I won't name the brokerage, but my brother and I have a string of restaurants and we have a fairly large sum that we wanted to invest. We approached this broker and we asked him what he thought of Wade Cook's strategies and he said, 'well I don't know who this Wade Cook guy is but he's doing stuff that only about 5% of us even know how to do, and it's the upper 5%.' "

WADE: But Wade Cook is a cab driver that happened to get on a platform. He got a microphone. Now he has best-selling books. Okay, I'm doing these, but when my book first came out, I was being criticized by everybody.

JOEL: Well, it's only the upper-echelon brokers that know what's going on.

WADE: Now I've got brokers, by the way, that will only let their students trade if they go through our training or read our books. My book has been a best seller, the Wall Street Money Machine. Now with, Stock Market Miracles, it's the same thing. It's got so many broker-related strategies, and like Wall Street Money Machine has to a certain extent been kept a best seller by stockbrokers buying 10, 15, 20 books at a time for all their clients. But there are still other stockbrokers who haven't read my books. They still criticize me.

KEVEN: The back end of that story is that they gave him a book, Wade.

WADE: They gave that stockbroker a book?

KEVEN: Yes.

WADE: Cool.

KEVEN: Now he knows who you are.

JOEL: It's awfully easy to be down on what you're not up on. That's cliche but it works.

WADE: All right, now, I want to deal with this word "diversify" for awhile. I just gave several strategies. To you, what is the difference between a formula, a strategy, or a method? I guess that "buy and hold" is a formula, but it's only one, right? I mean, when you do that you have to live by that. I guess what I'm after is making money, using the stock market to make money, to turn it into a business.

KEVEN: There are so many tools that it is incredible. We talk a lot about options at our workshop. Buying and selling options gives you so much leverage that you can turn a small movement in the market, or a particular stock, into a huge gain. In my mind, that gives you the knife that you can use to cut the rope between your little boat and this big ship that may be heading for the reef. So you go wherever you need to go.

RICH: But we're using formulas here. These formulas are something that have been proven, they have stood the test of time. They have worked before, they are working now, they'll keep on working in the future, no matter whether we're in a bull market, bear market, whatever. These are proven formulas.

WADE: We need to wrap this up, and I appreciate you being here. Everyone listening, just because we might, and I repeat, might, go into a bear market does not mean that you have to go into a bear market. You don't have to have a bear market mentality. There are always options, there are always opportunities, and there are always ways of making money, in good markets and in bad markets. I encourage you to be careful to whom you are listening. To come and join with our Team Wall Street, get on W.I.N.™, our computer Internet site, listen to our home study courses, watch our video courses. We are the number one, the premier financial educators in America. I often say, "We've got the best seminar in the country," but then I look around, and there's nobody in second place. There's nobody else even there. So I encourage you, right now, to pick up your phone, do not delay, it's going to cost some of you 10, 20, 30, 40,000 dollars a month to wait to take the Wall Street Workshop™. It's 800-872-7411. This has been Wade Cook with Rich Simmons, Joel Black, Pete O'Brien, and Keven Hart, hoping for you the best of futures. We wish you well and hope that you prosper, and if there's anything that our staff can do to help you make more money and keep more of what you make, that is what Stock Market Institute of Learning, Inc.™ is all about. Again, call 1-800-872-7411. Thank you for listening.

7

BUT WHEN?

Knowledge is of two kinds. We know a subject ourselves,
or we know where we can find information upon it
—Samuel Johnson

T here are two types of formats for determining stock values—both attempt to ascertain the movement of a stock's price. One is fundamental analysis and the other is technical analysis. I have weighted my decisions in favor of fundamental analysis, mostly out of personal bias. It just makes so much more sense to me. I have done well following, examining, and looking at the fundamental strengths (debt load, earnings per share, earnings strength, yield, and book value) of a particular stock. I've also studied these same aspects of the economy as a whole and even the market's different sectors. Looking at stocks, sectors, and the entire market from different paradigms is very enlightening.

I have also done well with certain aspects of technical analysis. It works well for looking at patterns (breakouts, DUCks, gaps, et cetera) for quick plays. Technical analysis helps determine more effective buy and sell points.

The technical area is where most bears incubate, or at least hibernate. Computer modules for guessing long-term movement are just not that accurate. Imagine software people getting together to figure out where the DOW will be in six months or a year. Their predictions, backed up by their software programs, have to be scrutinized carefully. Just a few well-placed "techs" can devastate a stock, or give credibility to one that should be ignored–yes, it has great technicals, according to point-and-figure charting, but lousy fundamentals.

THE FOUR HATED WORDS

Every time the market defies estimation, the cry is, "This time it's different!" These words are almost cliche. Are we in uncharted territory? Yes, there are some aspects of this marketplace which are the same as other periods, but we are where no market has been.

Prices of particular stocks are high, but not so for all companies. People are paying high multiples for some stocks, but 8 to 12 Price/Earnings can be found. There are some great bargains, but you have to look harder. There is no IPO fever, even though the volume is picking up. Earnings may have peaked in 1999, but many companies are poised, or have "plateaued," for a new surge. Inflation is down. The Fed is tinkering, but ever so slowly–trying to avoid both an increase in inflation and a recession.

> *Do your work with your whole heart and you will succeed–*
> *there is so little competition.*
> —ELBERT HUBBARD

As of late, interest rates have come down and have remained relatively low. It's uncanny as I reviewed every word of this book, written in the spring of 1997, the correctness of what I've ascertained then. The words written then were as prescient as any I've ever written.

Investor confidence is relatively high. This confidence could be seen as bearish, but several other indicators point to increases in production, exports, and growth.

So it could be seen as bearish, but there are just too many other good things happening in the economy to say this incredible bull cannot go on a little further. Baby boomers are getting older; many segments of the economy are truly solid. I'm going to ride the bull a bit longer.

Even many of these bearish technicians are turning optimistic. One says we'll be at DOW 12,000 this year. Some predict a 12,000 DOW by the year 2001 or 2002. One thought explains much of this. Some think that excessive bullishness is actually bearish. I don't have any empirical studies, but when the market crossed 11,000, it seems the proportion of bulls to bears (in market newsletters) was less than 50%. Everyone keeps thinking, or saying, "This has got to end." I don't view this situation as overly bullish. Yes it is bullish, but not overly so. Most bears, especially those in the closet, come out every time there is a run-up in stocks.

Obviously, the market never goes straight up. It never has, and it never will. There are many peaks and valleys along the way. Look at this chart of the DJIA. We see similar charts when we look at specific companies. The DOW is a range rider, a term I used in *Wall Street Money Machine, Volume 1* to show the ups and downs the market goes through. Most stocks, as they move up, do so in a similar manner. The market as a whole is a rolling stock, with an upward bias, a downward bias, or a flat or sideways bias.

•

Okay, let's get past the philosophical and get down to how to do plays in a bear market. Here are a few strategies to keep your mental life jackets above water:

Read everything you can get your hands on. Really study. Pay attention to signs that foretell market direction. Is it still going lower, or is it turning around? Just because stocks are in a bear market does not mean that you have to be in a bear market. There are always stocks that go up. Bear markets do not mean an end to volatility. Most of my strategies have their basis and strength in volatile stocks:

1. Write covered calls for income.

2. Play range riders, and in a bear market play reverse range riders.

3. Look for value and "dip"–buying opportunities.

4. Attend a Wall Street Workshop™. We have been, and will remain, on the cutting edge. Copycats abound, but we are unique in that we get nothing out of what you do. We offer pure education. You learn and you earn. Stock Market Institute

of Learning™ will have workshops, symposiums, and other forums. We won't stop helping people learn how to retire rich.

5. Be more careful. In an up market, everything works (except buying puts). In a down market, one has to be more selective.

6. Learn how to use charting services.

> *The first rule is not to lose. The second rule is not to forget the first rule.*
>
> —WARREN BUFFETT

7. Your entrance and exit points need to be defined better, therefore, technical analysis becomes much more important. If you don't want to learn the technical aspects yourself, then tap into services and newsletters that use them. More importantly, find a broker who loves the technical aspect of stock movements.

8. Base decisions on conflicting opinions. Do a lot of research, ponder, then ponder some more. Buy good companies with good P/Es, low debt, and diversified products.

9. Follow earnings. Companies with great earnings will be the last to go down and the first to recover.

10. Stick with the tried and true companies and methods for investing. Big company stocks are not always the best place to be, especially if earnings growth has slowed, and/or the price/ earnings ratio is really high. "Tried and true" means bread and butter industries with proven track records.

> *Imagination is more important than knowledge.*
>
> —ALBERT EINSTEIN

11. Follow closely (closer than in a bull market) news announcements. Watch for trends. When times are bad, everyone is

watching the news. Stick to the formulas that work, don't let temporary setbacks stop you from trading.

12. Don't panic. Waiting it out in today's fast-paced economics is time-honored advice you should employ–either in a bear market or on a serious correction.

13. Initial Public Offerings (IPOs) may not be the best place to be. Incidentally, IPOs slow down to famine levels during bear markets. If an IPO is on an existing company with good market share, low debt, and a history of profits, its IPO could do quite well. I avoid the highly speculative companies.

14. Diversify stocks. Build a portfolio of solid, proven winners. See *Wall Street Money Machine, Volume 2: Stock Market Miracles* for more information on this.

15. Diversify mutual funds. Not only pick a mutual fund which best reflects your needs, but own a variety of mutual funds. Many funds get hit hardest when there is a downturn. Why? Many own the same stocks. They all go in the entrance one at a time but then rush for a crowded exit when there is a panic. They own so much of certain stocks, when they unload major positions the price can be seriously driven down.

16. Diversify strategies. I've written about my 14 stock market strategies in other chapters and other books. *Wall Street Money Machine, Volume 1: Revised For The New Millennium, Volume 2: Stock Market Miracles,* and *Volume 4: Safety 1st Investing* teach these formulas. In times of negativism, dips, and recession, lighten up on the more aggressive plays. Still, study the fundamentals and play stocks and options in a reverse or downward-trending way. Be wise, be diversified.

17. Avoid any play with the number 13 in it. Just kidding. There are so many superstitions and other strange comparisons. It seems everyone has their favorite way to prove anything: invest

when the GOP wins; the second year of the second term of the President is always good; the 10:00 am to 11:00 am time period on Thursdays is the only time to invest, et cetera. I read these because they're amusing, but be leery of nonsensical advice. There are exceptions to every rule, including these observations. Besides, I get tired of changing the width of my ties to influence the markets.

The quality of a person's life is in direct proportion to their commitment to excellence, regardless of their chosen field of endeavor.

—VINCE LOMBARDI

18. Invest in companies with great management—bet on the jockey.

19. Stay focused on how to generate income when times get bad. Back up a little and take a hard look, make small forays (not only with stocks, but especially with options) into the marketplace. Monitor results, learn new rides, and keep practicing.

20. Be quicker at cutting losses than in a bull market. I dedicated a whole section of a chapter in *Wall Street Money Machine, Volume 2: Stock Market Miracles* to getting out of investments—especially coupled with the "why" of getting in. Simply put, it goes like this: how can you know when to sell if you do not know why you bought in the first place? Again, know your exit.

21. Long Term. If your strategy was to invest in a great company for the long term, than you should plan to live with the vicissitudes of the stock. Selling should take place after the story line has changed, either in your own life or in the life of the stock you own.

Don't be scared to take big steps—you can't cross a chasm in two small jumps.

                          —DAVID LLOYD GEORGE

22. Short Term. If your strategy is to generate cash flow, a quick in and out, then monitor your purchases more carefully. Put in sell orders when you purchase, and if it doesn't behave as expected, get out and move on. It either works or it doesn't. As Yoda says in *The Empire Strikes Back*: There is no try, there is only do.

23. Build a great support team. The people that love you the most may put you down the most. Sad, but true. Get those around you knowledgeable and up to speed. An uninformed mind is negative when confronted with new, (wild to them) strategies. Be careful whom you go to for advice.

8

MENTAL TRAPS

*When you reach for the stars, you may not get one, but
you won't come up with a handful of mud either.*

—LEO BURNETT

F ollow these ten steps and you are guaranteed to fail in the stock market. As a result, true poverty and frustration will be yours.

1. Don't diversify. Keep all your eggs in one basket. Keep life simple. Bet it all on red. Also, don't learn functional methods to increase your cash flow. Variety is not the spice of life. Anyway, you don't need more income, so exclusively stick with the "buy one stock and hang on" theory.

2. Don't read anything. There's so much weird stuff in the world, so what's the use? Don't seek out a diversity of opinions. There's too much information available—our minds are on information overload already. So, don't explore. Don't be concerned with the economic "signs of the times."

3. Look at past performance of stocks and invest in companies affected poorly by a recession or by negative conditions. Look for the worst, buy into the worst, be the worst.

4. Don't worry about income. You won't need more cash flow later so don't sell anything–including options (to generate income) on stocks you already own.

5. Don't worry about the quality of your stockbroker. Anyone will do. If they say or do negative things, follow them. If they bad mouth education, seminars, books, then follow their advice. If they want to be your only link to the world of profits, then go for it. Support the fact that they will be "down" on things that they're not "up" on. (Note: The author believes a good stockbroker can make you a fortune, but you've got to find and train him/her to be good). And don't think of having two stockbrokers. Who would want a second opinion or someone else finding good deals for you?

> *Beware of inside information...all inside information.*
> —JESSE LIVERMORE

6. Make sure you ask the opinion of everyone at work and church– especially those making $35,000 or less a year. They're tuned in to what's going on. Also, seek out people who know someone who lost their shirt in _____ (gold, stocks, business, and real estate). You fill in the blank. Avoid successful people.

7. Pay no attention to fundamentals (analysis). Ignore earnings– especially companies with increasing earnings. A company's debt is of no concern, so don't worry about it. Who cares about dividends and yields?

8. Play every insider tip you get. News from people "in the know" is very hard to come by. Shoot the wad on it. Who cares what they (whoever leaked the news, or made it up) have to gain by it?

9. Ignore temporary dips, or pullbacks. Remember, opportunity knocks only once. For you, it was when you were 23, so why look for more chances to make money now?

10. Don't educate yourself. It's a waste. Avoid the Wall Street Workshop™ at all cost. Who wants to learn how to double some of your money every two and a half to four months? Who wants to be retired in ten months? And anyway, who wants to be in a 40% tax bracket? Stay home and stay poor— let's not upset the apple cart. Whoever said, "You pay for education once, you continually pay for ignorance," just didn't know what they were talking about.

In a bear market, what's the difference between a stockbroker and a pigeon? The pigeon can still make a deposit on a BMW!

9

BE WISE

Obstacles are those frightening things you see when you take your eyes off the goal.

—HANNAH MORE

A common and integral part of my gold seminar is to encourage people to stay on the gold standard—at least to a certain extent. Just because America has gone off the gold standard does not mean that individual citizens should. A part of our assets should be in gold.

Now in my stock market seminars, I encourage people not to slip into a bear market mentality. Just because we enter a bear market does not mean all is lost. We can fight back. We can prepare. Our choices are varied and have profound consequences. One option is to sit out the bear downturn, wait, and get back in after the dip or crash is over.

I'll divide this section into two parts. The first part we'll deal with an overall bear market, the second part we'll deal with stocks which act like they're in a bear market, even though we're in a bull market.

DOWN MARKET STOCKS

Just because we enter a bear market does not mean that every stock goes down–or goes down dramatically. Some are recession-proof and some even fare very well. I'll make three general comments about finding good stocks in down markets.

1. News articles, but more specifically, magazine articles, are loaded with information about companies which fare well, or have fared well, in down markets. This genre of news proliferates during bad times. Major firms, and financial news sources go searching for values: bargain stocks, and stocks that fared well in previous downturns, or stocks that rebounded quickly. They usually comment on stocks with good upward potential. I remember these well in 1990 and 1991. Then again, in 1994. I thought, "What?" They're starting up again now. Even though times were good, a lot of the talk was bad. I won't list these stocks here. By the time the information is needed, the list would have changed. Don't worry, these sources are everywhere, and will become more widespread as we enter a bear market.

> *Evil news rides post, while good news waits.*
> —JOHN MILTON

2. There are a few firms that analyze stocks. Some over-analyze. Many stocks actually buck the trend of a downturn. These stocks are said to be "negative beta down" by the "techies." Let me explain. The beta of a stock is a measuring tool to see the volatility of a stock, or the likelihood of price changes, as measured against the movement in price of the underlying stocks. There is also a beta of the stock as compared to the Standard & Poors 500. For example, if a stock has a beta of 1.2, it is said to be .2 or 20% more volatile than the S&P. A beta of 2 would be a high flying, very volatile stock with a huge 2 X increase compared to the norm. A negative beta, say .8, is 20% less volatile the norm of 1. The model can get more sophisticated.

What if the market goes down and the stock has a negative beta? This is when a stock rises when the S&P goes down. A negative beta means the stock price increases in a down market. The analysis of "negative beta down" is extensive. I believe this information is valuable, if one is looking for stocks with good potential during down markets. Your stockbroker should be able to find reports on these companies. We could list several here but, once again, by the time you read this, the list would be out dated.

It's not difficult to find this information. We put these on W.I.N.™ when we find them (call 1-800-872-7411 to find out about our computer Internet service).

3. Good charting services can help you track stock performances, measure momentum, or buying power. You should subscribe to one of these services for current information.

Fortune is like the market, where many times, if you can stay a little, the price will fall.

—FRANCIS BACON

Up Market Stocks

In a bull market, many stocks do poorly. Some for no apparent reason whatsoever. I've made comments about a series of events leading up to a crash, a correction, or bear market. Sometimes these are a phenomenon and are difficult to explain. The same thing happens with individual stocks. Big dips (and big surges) just happen. Maybe because of program buying or selling. Maybe bad news (buying out the short sellers). Maybe competition. Sometimes the events are explainable; sometimes they're not. I went looking for stocks that recently had a 20% decrease (sometime more than six months to twelve months ago). Look at how they've performed. I've made comments where I thought appropriate. Remember, these down or "bear market" stocks occurred in a bull market.

There are two major points I'd like to make with this next part.

1. In up and down markets there are exceptions to the rule, or in other words, stocks that underperform or outperform the norm. It is finding these oddballs and either ignoring them or figuring out how to play them, which can make us money.

2. There are specific formulas, or methods, which can be employed to make money in any market. In down markets (actually, this usually means flat market after a serious decrease in value) there are companies which excel. Yes, it's tough to buck the trend but well managed companies not only do better, but they attract investors like a powerful magnet. The law of supply and demand takes hold and you have buyers choosing a few good stocks, driving the price up.

If you've followed the formulas given elsewhere in this book and throughout my other books, you would have been near the first to enter the picture, and in line to make substantial profits once the turnaround takes effect.

No rule is so general which admits not some exception.
—ROBERT BURTON

In up markets there are still companies doing poorly. Let's look at the chart of several of these companies with running commentary on how to play them. Please see range riders and reverse range riders in *Wall Street Money Machine, Volume 1: Revised For The New Millennium* and *Volume 2: Stock Market Miracles*. If you can learn how to play these now, think how much better off you'll be when the whole market acts like one of these stocks.

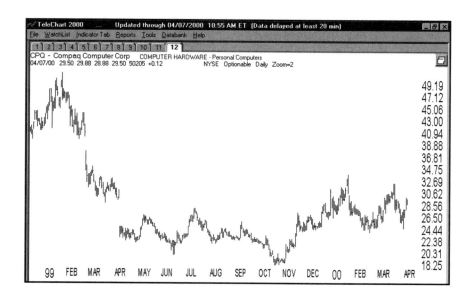

Compaq Computer, a widely held stock, and one that is frequently in the news, is our first candidate. In the beginning of 1999, the stock was near $50. In the spring of 1999 it was around $22. Look at the peaks and valleys. Too many opportunities for profits to list here. Look at the gap down in February, 1999, and the March/April 1999 gap down. Gaps are a tremendous play. Once the stock breaks out (up) or gaps down, the trend continues for the next few months (until more news comes out). This is more than a 50% decline in four months. With 20% one-to-one-and-a-half month down periods. (Note: Study range riders in *Wall Street Money Machine, Volume 1* and peaks and slams in *Volume 2: Stock Market Miracles*.)

From $30 to $24 in seconds. Now it's a rolling stock. Might this stock recover? Let me answer a question with a question. Isn't this a good time to check the fundamentals? Also, wouldn't you like to know why it fell in the first place–and then continued falling? Consider buying the $10 or $12.50 call option when the stock dips below $10. Buy them out at least two months to give it time to roll up–then get out with a 50¢ to 75¢ profit. Ten contracts would generate a profit of $500 to $750, with an estimated investment of $1,000. Also, consider selling puts when it's low and buying puts when it's high. Could be a good covered call stock.

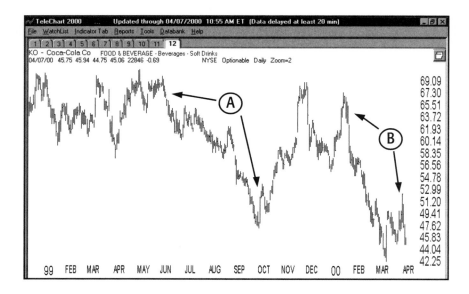

Now let's look at a chart on Coca-Cola Co. Look at the two sharp down turns, (A) and (B). This stock fell from $70 to $45 in 10 months. The Dow Jones Industrial Average was having a great year. Look at the number of times it fought to go back up. Has it established a new bottom? This might be a good one to check. Is it rolling? Is it turning around? Are the options expensive or cheap?

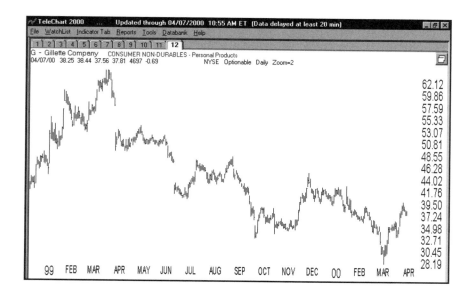

Gillette was in a strong uptrend during 1998. Then in 1999 it fell out of favor on Wall Street, losing about half its value. Find the bottom on this one.

> *We go the movies to be entertained, not to see rape, ransacking, pillage, and looting. We can get all that in the stock market.*
>
> —KENNEDY GAMMAGE

Look at the streakiness of this fall: from $20 to $9 in eight months. It looks like it's coming out of the doldrums—but not by much.

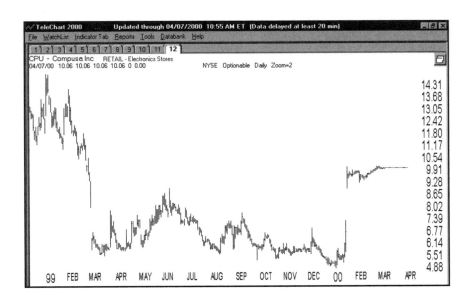

10

ANOTHER INTERVIEW WITH WADE

With enough inside information and a million dollars, you can go broke in a year.

—WARREN BUFFETT

T he following is a modified transcription of a heated panel discussion and interview between the host of Your Money Matters, John Childers, Cheryle Hamilton, and Wade Cook, author of numerous books, including *Wall Street Money Machine* and *Stock Market Miracles*. There is a powerful interaction going on. It's hard, it's fast and in quick-step time the listener, now you the reader, gets a useful earful of easy-to-implement ways to make money in any market, up or down.

This is John Childers from Your Money Matters and we have as our guest today Mr. Wade Cook, author of the *Wall Street Money Machine* Series and *Real Estate Money Machine*. You seem to have several books out here Wade and they all seem to be selling so well. Can you just tell our audience why your books are selling? In fact, even before you answer that, I want to know particularly about this book the *Wall Street Money Machine* Series. It seems like everyone who uses your methods is making money in the stock market. Why is everybody buying your books?

WADE: Well, I don't know if everybody is making money, and if they are making money, it may be that they're making money in terms of inflation–as in increasing stock value, but when you say "making money" to me–and that's exactly what my book is about–is that it helps people who are not so much interested in a stock or a mutual fund. I'm interested in helping people get in, get out, and make some cash, and when I say cash, I mean actual cash. Send it to the house, get a check, use that cash to buy other investments, use that cash to buy some real estate, support your family, go buy a new set of roller skates for your kids, I mean that's the kind of cash I'm talking about. So my book puts the emphasis on building up income.

JOHN: Well that seems to be a little bit different from what my broker is telling me. My broker is saying that if I just trust in him I should buy something and hold on to it and you're telling me something a little bit contrary to that.

WADE: Maybe the buy and hold method is okay for some people, and maybe that's okay for you. I don't ever give any recommendations. However, most people who really want to quit their job or quit their businesses just don't have the income to do so. The one thing they need to replace is income and by taking, say $5,000 or $10,000, and put it into IBM stock, they're out of control. You know, whether the stock goes up or down, whether the company pays a dividend or not, they're out of control. If the market is good and if inflation keeps in check and if interest rates stay low, then maybe their stock will do well, but it still doesn't provide any income. Maybe there will be a small dividend paid to them, but the amount necessary to live on would not be there.

CHERYLE: Wade, there is a lot of comment out in the financial world right now about the market going into a bear market. Your strategies are about cash flow and you're going about it in a bull market. How is this going to work in a bear market?

WADE: Well, obviously we can all take advantage of a bull market. Anybody can. It's hard to go wrong in a bull market. I mean you can buy almost any stock and it's going to go up in value. It's like swimming downstream with the fish. You're just going in the same direction—it's easy. It becomes tough when you change around and swim upstream. My point is, you play the market at hand. Whatever is there right now, that's the game that's in town, and that's the game you play.

Right now we're in the midst of a bull market and there is a lot of talk about a bear market. In a bear market, you just have to be more careful. You say, "What do I do?" Well, you put the emphasis on strategies. For example, you learn my rolling stock strategy or range rider strategy. In a bear market, these will change and become what we call a reverse range rider. Throughout my books, the *Wall Street Money Machine, Volume 2: Stock Market Miracles,* and at my live Wall Street Workshops™, we teach bear market strategies all the time: to diversify—to make sure that you don't have all your eggs in one basket. If you're doing options, for example, you buy some short-term options and some long-term options. You have in your portfolio certain stocks that you're in and out of. Some are like guerrilla warfare, you get in, you get out, and you make a lot of money. You also have other blue chip type stocks that you hold.

There's even a process called the "negative beta down." You can call your stockbrokers and say, "I want a list of stocks that go up when the market goes down." Now, a beta is a measurement of the volatility of a stock. Negative means the stock is going up in a down time. When you say "down," that means a down market, like a bear market is down. So negative beta down means that you can find stocks which go up when the market goes down. Knowledge is the key: knowing what to do in any marketplace.

CHERYLE: So, you're saying the same strategies you teach in your books and your seminars will provide the basis for playing a bear market and a bull market?

WADE: No, not necessarily. Some of my bull market strategies should be reversed. You do my strategies, but in reverse. For example, I'm really big into buying call options on stocks. In a bear market, you would buy puts as stock prices move down. In a bull market, you can just about buy anything, so the opposite strategy is this: you don't just buy anything, you need to be very selective. You do a lot more research. You get more into the technical figures like point and figure charting and other things like that. You find stockbrokers who are really good at technical analysis. The profits are going to be minimized unless you do extra homework. If you want more profits, then you have to be more careful in a bear market than you are in a bull market.

JOHN: It sounds to me that what you're teaching is different than what my broker has been telling me to do.

WADE: What has your broker been saying about a bear market?

JOHN: He tells me to buy and hold. What's bothering me, and I'm sure it's bothering our audience, is the fact that if you buy and hold and if a bear market takes over, we're going to be buying and holding as it's going down in value.

WADE: Right, and who wants to do that?

JOHN: It looks like you've got some different strategies here, and what I want to know is this: will your strategies protect me if things turn bad?

WADE: Well, if the market changes, it's not going to change that dramatically. There's no reason to believe a bear market is going to devastate anybody's portfolio for the long term. That has not been the case in the last 70 or 80 years. The only thing that affected the stock market, even at the time of the crash of 1929, was not so much the crash as it was stupid government policy. The Smoot-Hawley Tariff Act put up incredible trade barriers here and it had an affect around the world. It drove our economy into such a long-lasting recession. About the only thing that bailed us out of that recession was the Second World War. In 1987, for example, the stock market crashed. It literally crashed 30%. That crash, by the way, was in terms of percentage and dollar amounts, a lot more serious then the stock market crash of 1929, but it lasted around a year. For example, if you had $100,000 invested in 1987 and the stock market went down 30%, that means your investments went down to $70,000. But just a little under 13 months later, it was back up to $120,000.

Now, what if you had learned one of my strategies that would have had you buying on serious dips like that. You would have jumped in at $70,000 and ridden it back up to $120,000. You would have made a huge profit. Nevertheless, even if your existing portfolio had gone down, you still would not have lost. One of the things about bear market strategies is to not panic. Don't sell when everybody else is selling. You should buy when others are selling and you should sell when others are buying. When a stock makes a really high run up and everybody is jumping in on the momentum that may be the time to sell.

Back to 1987. If there's a huge crash, not only in the marketplace but in particular stocks, that may be the time to get in. Now, I'm not saying we're going to have a bear market or not. I'm saying we're not going to have a bear market now. Not now. Not this year, probably not next year, with interest rates in check and a Federal Reserve bent on making sure there is no inflation. This means they're going to keep a tight cap on interest rates and they'll raise or lower them a bit now and then to keep inflation down. If inflation is down and if the interest rates are down, and companies are doing well, earning a lot of money, then it does not point to a bear market. Now that's the point.

You know, we've never had anything like the serious dip of 1987 in the history of the stock market. Did the dip in the market affect the day to day operation of the companies? It may have affected a person's portfolio, but they're still driving down the street seeing Coca-Cola delivery trucks at 7-Elevens. Okay, so Coca-Cola stock went down $10, but the price of their products didn't go down $10. There's a world of difference between getting caught up in the negative sentiment in the stock market, but then you've got to walk outside and say, "Hey,

Ford is still selling cars. General Motors is still making cars. Microsoft is expanding overseas."

The everyday marketplace, the everyday running of America still goes on whether the stocks are up 100 points one day or down 100 points the next day.

What we have to learn is how to take advantage of the volatility. When a stock goes down $9 in one day, from $80 to $71, we jump on it and ride it back to $80. That's what we need to learn how to do, and that's what I teach in all my other books and now in my seminars: showing people how to look for opportunities. There are opportunities everywhere. Opportunity does not knock once, it knocks every day. And there are deals to be made every day.

JOHN: I'm kind of confused on an issue here. If you were giving us a list of companies we should invest in, I could understand why your books are selling like crazy. But you're telling us you don't give advice about which companies to buy and yet you're books are selling and you can't keep them in the bookstores. Why?

WADE: Because I don't give recommendations on certain companies. In my books, I do mention certain companies but only for illustrative purposes. I use particular companies as examples to show people a certain scenario of what might happen. We may put in charts to show patterns. What I am into is formulas. I'll give several of them. Rolling stock–where you find a stock that trades between a certain range. It goes from $2 up to $3 and back down. Another formula is range riders where a stock will go from $70 up to $77, then back to $72, then up to $80. It's on a climb, say from $70 up to $100, but it's not a straight shot. So it goes from $70 up to $77, and then backs off to $72. The next time it goes up to $80, but it goes back down to $73, three or four weeks later. And every time it makes a dip back down, you ascertain the bottom, which is not tough to do, and then you buy it right there, or buy options on it right there. And then when it hits a new high and starts to back off, then we sell it. It peaks out and it comes right back down.

That's called Range Riders. That's the name I made up for this movement.

How about writing covered calls, or buying stocks that are on serious dips? I mean talk about bear market mentality. My whole covered call scenario is about buying stocks on dips and then selling options on those stocks to generate income. Another strategy is to sell puts. Selling puts is where you agree to buy stock at a certain price and you sell puts when you think the stock is going to go up. So when a stock is low, you buy a call option and you sell a put option. When a stock is high, you sell a call option and you buy a put option. Now I've outlined this in Stock Market Miracles under tandem plays, doing two plays while the stock goes up and then two plays while the stock comes down. Now you have some people who say, "You can make money in any market," I say, "Not only can you make money in any market, you can make money twice when the stock is going up and twice when the stock is going down, if you know how to play them."

CHERYLE: This incredible enthusiasm and optimism in the face of what we're learning is exciting for the people who are listening, but we're all affected by the media, and hearing all of these negative things, how do we avoid all this negativism?

WADE: That's a great question. You've got to keep things in perspective. Let me give you an example. This morning before we did this interview, I was reading an article. Listen to what it said, then I'll turn this interview around and ask for your response. It said this: when they started doing the Dow Jones Industrial Average, basically from the beginning the stock market was formed, it took 88 years for the Dow Jones Industrial Average to get to the 1,000 level. Now, the Dow Jones Industrial Average is a blending of thirty different companies on a weighted average of their stock prices. It took 88 years to get to 1,000, but it took from November of 1996 until February of 1997 for it to go from 6,000 to 7,000. It went up 1,000 points in four months. Did you catch that? 1,000 points in four months. It went 1,000 points in 88 years, and now, it went 1,000 points in four months and people are saying, "That's too fast–1,000 points in four months." So when some read this they say, "Wow, we're ripe for a crash because it's gone up too fast." What's your response? What do you think? What this article was trying to say was, "Watch out everyone. We've got a crash coming."

JOHN: Well, my response would be, I need to know more about the market, learn why these things are about to happen and what I should do with my money.

WADE: Are you scared by hearing that though?

JOHN: Well, a little bit.

WADE: OK. What do you think?

CHERYLE: Actually, it makes me more curious. I think I would want to get more involved in trying to figure out really how can I profit myself. How can I prepare my portfolio so I can be crash proof, so to speak?

WADE: OK, I think that was the intent of the article. That's what they wanted to do. Make people think they need to have a better mix of stocks, or get out of the market. But not me. You see, I look at the 88 years for it to go from zero to 1,000. Well, look at the percentage. To go from 6,000 points up to 7,000 points, what's that? That's about a 17% growth rate. So 17% of 6,000 would be 1,000. There's a 17% difference between 6,000 and 7,000. What is the percent difference between zero and 1,000?

CHERYLE: 1,000%.

WADE: See the point? So it took 88 years. Now if they went back and said it took two years for it to go from zero to 100 then that would make more sense, right? They use 88 years, but it had to go clear from zero. The percentage rate of growth to get from zero to 1,000 is absolutely so much more remarkable. It is much more phenomenal going from 6,000 to 7,000 in four months. But when you put what people are saying and what the market is doing in perspective you say, "This movement is not that bad of a deal. You know, it's not that great of a rate of return."

CHERYLE: No. You're looking at 15 to 17%.

WADE: The last couple of years it's been around 20%.

CHERYLE: It's up a little better than average but it's not phenomenally different.

WADE: That's right. That's the point, to answer your question. You've got to keep it in perspective; is this really that high, outlandish, or weird? Your question was how do you deal with all the negativism. You've got to look at the intent of that statement being made. So, I look down at the end of the article and sure enough there was the name of a financial planner in some city selling his services. Fear sells. What's their intent? Their intent is to sell a newsletter. Their intent is to pick you up as a new investor so you'll spend all of your money with them, so they can make commissions off of all your investments. You see, and to answer your question about my seminars, I get nothing out of what people do. I don't want their money. I don't invest their money. I don't make recommendations on their money. I want to teach strategies, and the people keep all their own profits. I'll show them how to keep everything in perspective. I'll show them how to work the formulas. I'll show them how to make the money. They get to keep all of their profits and that's the big difference between me and everyone else.

JOHN: I'd like to change the subject here, Wade. It sounds like you know a lot about your stock market strategies. You've written extensively about them. I'm sure you've made a lot of money, but for our listening audience, the average, hard working person, what does this all mean to them? What does it mean to those who are just getting started?

WADE: Let me give you several things people can do to get them on the road to wealth right now.

1. Currently, we are in the middle of a bull market. Play the market at hand. Don't get caught up in the pessimism that there might be a bear market or that you should bullet proof yourself as much as possible. You should be buying your investment in entities that pay no taxes. For example, bombproof your investments in legal entities like Nevada Corporations, Living Trusts, Pension Plans, et cetera. In fact, I have an entity structuring tape cassette seminar that I'll send anyone for free. Just call 1-800-872-7411. It's called the Entity Structuring tape.

2. You ought to be buying stocks and also diversify your portfolio, not only into real estate or other business interests, but into stocks that are diversified—even blue chip stocks that hold up well in bad times. I have a subpart to number two. The problem with what I just said is that a lot of people listening right now would like to do more, not only buy more, but buy better investments. They don't have the cash to do it, so if they scrape together $10,000 and put it into Coca-Cola or IBM, their money is tied up. What I've tried to show people at my seminars is a way to use the stock market itself as a business. Buy and sell, buy and sell, get in, get out, make a profit. Then take some of your profits and keep it moving. Take some and buy other great investments like these blue chip stocks.

   Another part of number two would be to buy investments that hold up well. Do research to find stock and other investments that are recession proof. There are a lot of companies that do well in bad times. They just are not affected by recessions. Some thrive in recessionary times. You definitely want to have some of those in your portfolio.

3. You want to buy stocks that are widely traded. You want to avoid little no name stocks. So in a bear market you want to have stocks that everybody else wants to own. In real estate,

we used to teach people to get in the way of progress. You know, buy a piece of ground where the mall is going. Try to guess where the freeways are going to go.

In the stock market the way you get in the way of progress is to invest in companies that all these big mutual funds will want to invest in. Think about it. They've got to invest. For example, one place to invest would be into the Dow Jones Industrial stocks themselves, or into any of the 500 stocks in the S & P 500. Why? Because huge mutual funds have billions of dollars, some trillions of dollars, that have to be invested in just those stocks.

For example, a couple months before this interview one of the companies got dropped out of the S & P 500. The S & P 500 added Conseco, the ticker symbol CNC. The stock went up $5 to $6 within a couple of weeks. Why? Because many of these mutual funds have to buy that stock. They had to get rid of the stock in the company that was dropped from the 500 and buy the Conseco stock. They have to own it. They're index funds. They own all the stocks in a particular index. You get in the way of progress by owning stocks that everybody else wants to (or needs to) own.

4.   You want to make sure that you find a good stockbroker. Somebody who can really educate you. Somebody who is a little bullish on the marketplace, or is at least bullish on education and knowledge. Somebody who has a good computer system and who can track stocks well for you; someone who can get research reports for you, tracking services and things like that. It basically comes down to not only what you know, but also who you know.

5.   And the last point is to get educated. I mean, I don't care what area people are interested in doing, they need to come to my seminars or someone's seminars. If they don't come to mine, they've got to go somewhere but, you know, the somewhere

else doesn't exist. I want to say we have the best (Wall Street Workshop™) in the whole country and I turn and look around and there's nobody else in second place. We have the only seminar that teaches people on a hands-on, experiential basis how to do deals and work formulas. We teach people how to get results.

We get people so excited about making money, indeed actually making money that they'll take a portfolio of $10,000 and turn it into $30,000 in a matter of months. Triple their money. Now, think this one through. If they now have $30,000 and there's a stock market crash, are they better off? Let me make a quick point about stock market crashes. I don't see a bear market around the corner anywhere near us right now. But could there be a stock market crash? Yes. A 10, 20, or 30% dip? Yes. We keep having little corrections. We need these. These corrections are really nice. Down 90 points in one day and then it climbs back up over the next week. It's not bad, but a consolidation time. A time for some to take their profits. A time to recover. But look at the strength (the breadth and depth) in the current market. We have a new concern, something they didn't have in 1929 called Program Trading. For example, a lot of funds have computer which triggers a sale when stocks his a certain price. All of a sudden, orders are flying. When a lot of the same funds own the same stock and start selling them, all of a sudden the stock goes down to $80 almost overnight. In total this action could cause a stock market crash.

Also two points on that. Number one, obviously we want to avoid stocks that the major funds own. This is different than buy the stocks we like which are also listed in a particular index. We want to be diversified. Number two, we want to take advantage of dips. So always have some money on hand. Always. That's one of the things we teach at our seminars. Have some cash ready to take advantage of opportunities. Don't spend all your money right now. Keep some in reserve so you can jump in on these really serious dips in the marketplace.

JOHN: I don't mean to put you on the spot, but maybe I do because I think I owe it to our listeners to ask you this. These people who are coming to your seminars, are they really making money?

WADE: They really are making money. They are buying new cars. They're putting down payments on houses. We had one guy that we just heard of on the Internet the other day who started with $20,000. In about six and a half or seven months, he was over $300,000. A guy came with $30,000 and made over $700,000 in five months. I can't even read all the letters anymore, all the testimonials. We show people how to make money. We tell them, we show them, and then we have them actually do it. Now many people make money right during the class. I mean the cost of the seminar is made back, sometimes even more. Some of the people make back the cost of the seminar right in the class. However, our emphasis in teaching is to show people how to practice perfectly so when it's time for them to use real money they're ready.

The emphasis is on making money. After the class is over they just keep it going. They learn a formula, it's repetition, it's duplication, and they just turn it into a machine. One person may come and really like rolling stocks. Another person comes and really likes covered calls. By the way, most people really like covered calls. That's one of the top strategies that people use after the course—writing covered calls. Other people love selling puts and others like range rider strategies. They pick the one that they like. They get to be an expert in that one, and then they use it repetitiously.

So my point is, you gotta make hay while the bull climbs. Play the market at hand. It's climbing right now. You take somebody that has $10,000, they run it up to $100,000 in even six months or nine months or a year, and then if there's a 10 or 20% decline, what do they have? And wouldn't you rather have a 10% decline on $100,000? OK, so you're only worth $90,000. So big deal. You started with $10,000 a year ago and now you're worth $90,000. Even if you're down to $70,000, you're still a lot better off. You've got to keep everything in perspective and not get caught up in all the negativism.

CHERYLE: You're making it sound like it's just as exciting to play a bear market as it would be to play a bull market.

WADE: It would be. Because the strategies, even though they're different, will be pretty much the same, although some will be reversed. You have to be a lot more careful and use the technicals. I'm sure that both of you have had times in your life when you were a lot more flush than you might be right now, or maybe much worse. You know, you lost your job or something and you go to the grocery store, and you shop better. It's the same thing in the stock market. When you only have a little bit of money and your money has to go a long way, you're just more careful on how you shop. When everything is going well, when you've got a full box of soap to do your laundry, you use any amount you want. But when there's only one scoop left in the bottom of the box you start rationing–using half scoops. You're just more careful. You make do. You adjust.

CHERYLE: So this sounds like making lemonade out of lemons.

WADE: It is exactly that. Again, though, there are some people who are always going to be negative. And I'm asking everyone who is listening to this interview right now to not worry about that so much. Use this negativism that's in the marketplace for your benefit. It's kind of like keeping a check on runaway inflation. It keeps a check on the market.

There's a lot of program trading that goes on. There's a lot of profit taking that goes on. A stock goes from $60 up to $90 and people say, "I'm happy here." If it hits $100 then a lot of people sell it. Well, all that selling activity drives the stock back down to $90. That's when we can jump in and take advantage of it, when it hits a new bottom. We need the bears with us. We need people out there talking negative. I don't want them to go away. I just want the people listening right now to keep it in perspective and to realize what they're after. A lot of people get so negative–they think a stock is going to go down so they short sell the stock. Then you see them bad mouthing the stock because they want the price of the stock to fall. That's why I've never been big on short selling. It changes your mental attitude. I don't want to be constantly thinking about things going down.

We as Americans, in this rugged individualistic country, have a driving need to grow and to thrive. So do companies. The drive takes on a life of its own. Many companies want to grow, to expand, to do better, and to build in quality. As long as that drive exists in America, (and who says that it will ever go away) I want to invest here.

Remember a couple years ago when everybody said, "Well American productivity is down compared to the Japanese and the Germans." Hogwash! We came back and beat their butts. We are so much better in our productive hours right now than anybody. We are the country that everybody is coming to. We are the country where all the money is coming. We may have slumps from time to time, but this is the country that has an incredible attitude. So this is where we need to be and we don't need to be ashamed or afraid. I guess the point I'm trying to make is this: just because the stock market might go into a bear market phase, does not mean that anybody listening to this, any of our students, has to be in a bear market mentality.

I know I've said this in all of my seminars. Realize that the average bull market lasts three to five years. The average bear market lasts about nine months. The last one was only six months in 1990. The teddy bear of 1998 lasted 2 1/2 months. Compare bulls of three to five years to nine-month bears. Think of the comparison. And there are three bull markets for every one bear market. What should you be gearing your strategies to? So what if there's a bear market? Go on vacation for six months or nine months. Then come back and play the next bull market.

CHERYLE: You know, you have just provided the confidence I need now to start working with these strategies. Often times I'm hearing, "That's fine, but what happens if I get into trouble? How do I work with it? I don't feel like I can afford this." You're telling me now that I have the ability to work with these strategies in a way that allows me to continue on. It's not going to impede me. I'm not going to lose money just because the economy decides to take a turn.

WADE: You may lose money on any particular deal, but you won't lose money overall. Not if you keep a long term perspective and you keep using your profits in your short term deals to buy (long term) better stocks. And even if you have a stock that you bought at $60, like a Coca-Cola, and it runs up to $90 or $100 and then goes back to $80, your $60 is still $80. What if you started with $10,000 and in a year or two you built it up to $200,000 and now your money is in better stocks. Then the stocks go from $200,000 to $250,000. All right? Then there's a 30% drop back down to $175,000. So what? You see, you've got to keep it in perspective. Nobody wants to see those kinds of drops but you shouldn't be panicking just because there's a dip in the market-place or a crash—mini-crash or a maxi-crash. You should not panic. That's one of the mental things you have to keep up on, there's always tomorrow. Hey, that sounds like a Broadway show.

JOHN: Well, I'm excited! I know Cheryle is excited and our audi-ence is probably excited. What do we do from here? What steps do we take starting right now?

WADE: You get in the marketplace. You open up your brokerage account. Hopefully you'll come to one of my seminars and get edu-cated. Read my books. Get other books. Go to every bookstore and buy every book on the stock market you can. Keep it in perspective. Remember we need the bears. Read about bear market strategies, but start doing something. Start now. Take $500, take $1,000, and start doing something. You're going to learn by experience (that's what we do at the Wall Street Workshops™ is teach people by experience), but the most important thing right now is to start doing something. Just get $500 or $1,000, $5,000, or $10,000 invested and get that money moving and turning and making profits to buy more and better invest-ments for tomorrow.

JOHN: Thank you very much Mr. Cook.

11

WRAP UP

Man's mind, once stretched by a new idea, never regains its original dimensions.

—OLIVER WENDELL HOLMES

Everywhere a cacophony of sounds emanate. You'd think that the bear market was already upon us. However, many people who have been listening to these emanations from seemingly knowledgeable sources have missed out on some of the most tremendous gains in stock market history.

The market crash of 1987, a nearly 30% drop, has become a new benchmark for a serious correction or major dip in the marketplace. That dip, that correction, was a lot more than the stock market crash of 1929, both in terms of percentages and in terms of dollar amount. I remember seeing numerous people on TV wailing and moaning about the loss of their pension money. I'm also sure that their financial planners and other financial professionals were telling them to go ahead and sell because it may even go down more. While it may be true in some cases that cutting your losses is good advice, it sure was not true in this case. Any person with any money sense at all would have realized that this was a buying opportunity, and not a time to sell.

One of the answers to the question we receive about knowing when to sell is to only sell when you would not buy. Could not this strategy be used in reverse—you should not sell when you should consider buying? It's pretty much the opposite side of the same coin. When there are swings in the marketplace and/or peaks and valleys in any particular stock's climb, which points to a formula for buying on dips and selling on strength. You would look to buy on dips in the stock price or when the whole marketplace is down.

> *When the prices are high they want to buy; when the prices are low they let them go.*
>
> —IAN NOTLEY

It is my firm contention that we are not soon headed into a bear market. I know that this is good news for a lot of people and it is my best educated guess after looking at several stock market and economic scenarios. I do not contend that I am an expert as an economist in the marketplace in general. I am an earnest investor, a dedicated observer, a cash flow practitioner, and a concerned citizen.

This concern has led me to the belief that tens of thousands, possibly millions, of people are getting bad advice and have sat out one of the largest stock market rallies in the history of mankind. Why? Because it seems like pessimism prevails everywhere. I say this tongue in cheek because to me optimism is the key to success. Do not bet on pessimistic statements, do not gamble on negative people, and surely do not invest your mental energy in gutter dwelling comments. There are so many opportunities to make money both in up markets and in down markets. We have to explored some of those possibilities in this short book and hopefully show the readers many ways to not only make money but also how to mitigate any losses on any dips in the market.

My books, *Wall Street Money Machine, Volume 1*, and now *Volume 2: Stock Market Miracles* have been so popular because they give people hope and actual strategies that create actual cash flow. I want you to read a letter I received from a surgeon.

> *Dear Wade:*
>
> *I wish to thank you for your wonderful contributions. I'm writing not only to express my gratefulness, but to share an experience I had about two weeks ago that has more to do with the human experience than directly with financial success. On a Friday your tape arrived and I was wondering when I was going to find the time to listen to it. At 1:00 A.M. that very next morning there was an emergency call for me (I am a practicing vascular surgeon of 20 years). And I was groggily dreading another sleep-deprived weekend. On the way to the hospital, I heard most of the new tape, and was amazed at the transformation of how I felt. By now I was fully awake, alert, refreshed, and eagerly anticipating what lay in store.*
>
> *I now realize what took place. You gave me something very important that early morning. That something is HOPE. Hope, one of our most powerful emotions, is the essence of motivation, and is priceless. Hope means different things to different people, but to me it means the promise of a less demanding professional life, of a life actually being with my family, of being able to retire from medicine rather than being retired by it, of financial security in essence. Hope is the future!*
>
> *I profoundly thank you for rekindling that spirit that is within us all. Moreover, you are providing the power through which hope is operative. That power is EDUCATION, that engine we need to move us forward. Education is inestimable and irredeemable. You have that unique ability to make complex matters seem readily comprehensible. As a surgical educator I know what a*

rare gift this is. Again, I thank you for sharing your special talents.

–J.K., M.D., OR

I had no idea that my methods would have such a dramatic impact in peoples' lives. This is a beautiful letter. I do not get many as articulate and eloquent as this, but I do get hundreds of letters and testimonials every week from people who have been through my seminars and who are now living better lives.

Let me tell you a story about what happened to one of our instructors. The other night he had a visitor in his home and when the man found out that he did financial seminars he berated the stock market in many ways. He brought out all the negative ideas about risk. He paraphrased (but thought he was quoting) many financial gurus. Obviously he was taking bits and pieces of different scenarios and different comments and putting them together into the most awful future scenario he could muster. This person was so wedded in negativism that our instructor had a really hard time getting a word in edgewise, let alone being able to rationalize with this man.

> *If the models are telling you to sell, sell, sell, but only buyers are out there, don't be a jerk. Buy!*
>
> —WILLIAM SILBER

Finally, when the man was almost out of steam and after having said several of his sentences redundantly, our instructor was able to get a word in. And here was a simple scenario that he gave. "I am making about 40% a year on my money. (Actually he's doing better than that, but negative people surely don't want to hear good news.) Over the last two years, my $100,000 has grown from $100,000 to $140,00 to over $180,000. So, if there is a 10 to 20% dip in the marketplace and I go back to $150,000, am I not a lot better off to invest while the market is good, to run up my profits to the highest level that I possibly can, and then if there ever is a downturn in the market I'll be much better off than having my money sit this one out? Won't I be much better off than if I have my money in a bank account?" Finally the man had no answer.

I'm going to propose the same situation here: What will it be like if you do not participate in this stock market rally? Take what profits you can, play the economy, play the market for all that it is worth. Use cash flow strategies to build up your income, but then take this income and build up your asset base. And don't panic.

If you don't profit from your mistakes, someone else will.

—YALE HIRSCH

1

WHY W.I.N.™?

Chance favors the informed mind.

—LOUIS PASTEUR

One way to keep up your optimism is to hang out with Wade Cook and his Team Wall Street every day. While you obviously can't be with this power-packed group of men and women physically, they have created a computer Internet service where you can see what they are doing. This incredible service is called W.I.N.™, or Wealth Information Network™. To sign up and learn more about other opportunities that are available to you, call Stock Market Institute of Learning, Inc.™ at 1-800-872-7411.

Following are very brief examples of what Wade Cook and Team Wall Street have shared on W.I.N.™ over the course of the last year. Most of the information put on W.I.N.™ is real examples of real trades and the results. These clips are solely to show what Wade Cook and the Team Wall Street have been saying.

Before we list some of what's been said, let's hear what one stockbroker had to say:

> *Dear Wade:*
>
> *I figured the small investment for your book, Wall Street Money Machine, would be worth the risk. I was so impressed that I subscribed to the W.I.N.™ bulletin board service. Now my life has changed forever!*
>
> *An example of one of my first investments was in Sybase Inc. (SYBS). I purchased 300 shares on October 2, 1996 and then sold 3 covered call contracts on them and was called out on October 18, 1996. My return was 23.73% in 16 days or a 534% annualized return.*
>
> *Wade you are a God send. Thank you for providing the tools and information to really make money and have more time for church and family.*
>
> SINCERELY,
CHUCK L.

MARCH 4, 1999

Good morning everyone, this is Wade.

I just got done playing basketball, and I was really looking into a lot of different plays. I am looking at Dell Computer (DELL), Microsoft (MSFT), and the deal going on with Dell and International Business Machines (IBM), and the new AT&T (T) and America Online (AOL) deal.

I just put in an order to buy 200 shares of America Online (AOL) at $82. I will make some more comments on that later on.

I also looked at Ford Motor Company (F), if you look a chart it could go down to $56 or so, but it looks as though it is in a roll pattern between the high $50 and mid $60 range. I bought 10 contracts of the

June $55 calls for $6^1/$_4$, and 10 contracts of the September $60 calls for $5^1/$_2$. I put in an order to sell them at $4 more that the purchase prices. I already have my order to sell in right now.

I did a similar trade on Compaq (CPQ). I bought 10 contracts of the July $30 calls for $7^1/$_8$, and 10 contracts of the October $35 calls for $5^7/$_8$.

I want to make a few comments on some of the research that we are doing. This will take awhile, and I am going to make this a part of my new book Safety First Investing, on noticing patterns in the quarterly report filing scenario. It seems to me that a lot of these stocks are driven by news. I am dividing news into two categories: internal news and external news. Internal news is news that is put out from the company, stock split announcements, mergers, share buybacks, earnings reports, dividend increases or payouts, those usually happen in a set pattern. The external news is analysts' recommendations, rumors of a merger, things that are driven from the outside about the company. The internal news from the company seems to go in this quarterly cycle, where if the quarter is ending on March 31, about mid-March, if the sales are down or earnings will not meet expectations, someone from the company will come out and announce this. The company has 45 days to do their SEC filings, from March 31 until May 15, there is a lot of newsy type periods. They do not have to wait for 45 days, but lets just say that they wait until the end of the quarter, March 31, and then five weeks later there are more and more rumors of what the earnings are going to be. There is another go round of the news. The stock may have dipped a little on the mid-March negative announcement, and then the stock will rally or not rally depending on the type of expected news coming out, from the middle of March on up to the end of March. And then when the news actually does come out, if there has been a lot of high expectations for the earnings, there is a dip in the stock at the time. I do not know if you have noticed the same thing, that is just an observation on my part. It seems to happen so much, I have my Research Department taking 30 companies on the Dow and 50 companies on the S & P 500, and we are taking a year back report look at what happened on these things, to see if we can notice some definite trends. If my surmising is correct, or even close, this gives us many opportunities to play and many things to be careful of.

For example, mid-January, when all the news came out about the stock splits and earnings about a lot of these companies like International Business Machines (IBM), Intel (INTC), Microsoft (MSFT), Dell Computer (DELL), Sun Microsystems (SUNW), McDonalds (MCD), Xerox (XRX), all these companies, and everyone wonders why the stock goes back down. Well, one of the reasons that I am seeing is that there is no news. The news cycle seems to have extended itself, its gone, and we need to wait another 30 to 45 days to get back into the next myriad of newsy go-round. I see this pattern a lot, and I am trying with more acute powers of observation see it, watch it, notice it, and see if there are any trades that we can do to play on it.

We will keep you posted on our research on this, but you may want to start watching these things yourself.

That is all for now!

(Note: Wade has completed his news–no news research and has made his dynamic findings available in a home study course. Yes, Red Light, Green Light is now available. Contact an enrollment representative at 1-800-872-7411 to learn more about Red Light, Green Light.)

DECEMBER 9, 1998
Good morning everyone, this is Wade:

I just got out from playing basketball, and I was thinking about some of the positions we have on Amazon.com (AMZN). We have a couple of Bull Put Spreads which are working very well for us with the stock up over $200. The stock was up $4 or $5 today and is coming up on its January 4, 1999 3:1 stock split, so it appears to have a lot of upward momentum. My Trading Department was telling me there is a really heavy support level at around the $180 range. Obviously, that is historical and doesn't mean it is going to hold that in the future, but it looks good at the $180 range. So, I was just calling up and looking at doing some $170/$180 Bull Put Spreads. Now this type of a spread, we are going sell the December $180 puts and buy the $170 puts to protect our downside and to limit our margin requirement, and in this case here if you did 10 contracts, that would be $10,000, but we're going to pick up $1 on that. So, you pick up $1, with 10 contracts that would be $1,000, and you have $10,000 on hold but you also get credit for that $1, which the market gave you. You know, the market put that $1 into your account. So you have basically $9,000 on hold. Here it is Wednesday, and we're talking, you know, these are going to expire next Friday. As long as Amazon.com (AMZN) stays above $180 through next Friday, we are just fine on this one.

Now, while I was discussing that, we were looking through the account, you know, a different account, and I had some Amazon.com (AMZN) $150/$160 December Bull Put Spreads. Now once again, I sold the $160s and bought the $150s, and I did it for a $2 net credit on that one, which was, you know, again, a $10 spread to net $2. I did this one several weeks ago. So I looked at the stock being clear out $210 right now, and in a $150/$160 Bull Put Spread, I am safe as long as the stock stay above $160. But then I started thinking, I wonder what I could wind out of this position for. In other words, what would it cost me to end this $150/$160 Bull Put Spread. And then a lot of you are going to say, "well why would you end it with the expiration date just 10 days away, why not let the thing expire," because as long as the stock stays above $160, it is going to expire and I just keep all the money we made. But then again, I made $2 on the spread when I sold that. I sold the $160s for $8³/₈ and bought the $150s for $6³/₈, so that netted $2 or $2,000. I actually did 20 contracts, so that is $16,000 on hold to make $4,000. Not a bad deal. But right now, I can buy back the $160s and sell the $150s and it would cost me ¹/₄ x ³/₈! So that would be $500 up to $650 to end the position. Now once again, why would I want to do that? Simply to free up the margin. In one case, I made $4,000 and tying up $16,000. Now, somewhere between $500 and $650, is tying up the same $16,000 in margin requirements. So where $4,000 as a return on $16,000 is pretty cool, you know, $500 to

$650 is not good at all! So why not just end the position and free up the money and get the money working better elsewhere?

So while I was there in that account, I checked on the December $180/$190 Bull Put Spread, but I don't have the confirmation yet on this one. I think I was picking up $2 on that one. We are going to spend $1/4$ x $3/8$ times the 20 contracts to get out of one position. And I don't want anyone to think that these have to be married together. I am not getting out of the one position so I could get in to the other position, but some of you might have to do that. For example, you've got basically $16,000 margin on hold and it stays tied up for $500 to $650. In case you don't understand that, I will explain it. We have .25¢, times 20 contracts, would be $500. Or $3/8$, times 20 contracts, would be $650. So, if I am going to leave that position there, I am tying up basically $16,000 to $20,000 in margin for $500+, and I could just sell it and get out of that position, and get in to another position at net about $2, and have another $4,000 profit with a $16,000 to $20,000 margin hold in the account. Hopefully this is all understandable; if its not, you should be working with a good stockbroker who really understands options and loves doing options, particularly spreads. And once again as a reminder, you don't have to do them in 20 contract matches, but the market makers really like that quantity. You could do 3, you know, sells and buys on a Bull Put Spread or Bull Call Spread, but they really like the 20 contract deal. It may be better to do 20 of a $5 spread if you can't afford to do 20 of the $10 spread. In these upper prices like Yahoo! (YHOO), Amazon.com (AMZN) and even Intel (INTC) now, you may want to look at the $10 spread.

Another newsy announcement, there is a new index on Internet stocks that has just started. I don't know that much about it, you may want to check it out. It opened up around $350 and is already up $4 on the day. You can buy options, you know, calls and puts on this index. It is an equally weighted index. The ticker symbol is DOT and I don't know that much about it. I just wanted to pass this along as a news item. The options on it right now are very, very expensive. For example, the December $350 calls are like $15, so they look very heavily priced.

NOVEMBER 23, 1998
Good morning, this is Wade:

Here's wishing you an early Merry Christmas and a happy holiday season. I was thinking long and heavy this weekend about this current stock market and, you know, how to play it and the direction to take. I always have a hard time when I think about the market going up and up and up, and trying to find buying opportunities. We always get little pull backs either in the market or a stock and jump back in. As there is talk around the Northwest right now about Eagle Hardware & Garden (EAGL) being taken over. The big talk all around the country is about this deal between America Online (AOL) and Netscape (NSCP) and some marketing arrangements with Sun Microsystems (SUNW). So let me address the market in general for a few minutes and I hope you can take this for what it is worth, you know, take my opinion and my commentary and mix them with all the opinions and commentary you receive and come up with a strategy of your own for playing this current market place.

I believe right now that there is so much strength in the market that we are going to see quite a substantial rise over the next little while. One of the reasons for this is that the market direction has just turned around so quickly from people being bearish to now people being bullish. And the fact is that there are literally billions upon billions of dollars sitting in the wings, waiting to come back into the marketplace. There are newsletters and industry reports and analyst reports encouraging people to be fully invested once again and virtually some of them, the ones I read, have been telling people to not have any money in cash , and to get it all back into the market. You know you can take that information for what its worth, that's not my feeling, but I am just pointing out that there are so much ailing sentiment right now and with all this cash waiting to get back invested, and that's cash sitting in mutual funds, cash that is sitting in investors accounts and pension accounts, and there is just a lot of cash available to match up with the demand for the market place. I don't know if the market is going to go to 10,000 or 11,000 in the first quarter like some people are saying. That's not my strategy anyway. My strategy is to find good buying/selling opportunities: open positions and close positions for a small part of your portfolio to have it in the cash generation machine, and what we need is this simple mentality in even a nice neutral marketplace and we can still make a lot of money. When I say make a lot of money this is cash money. You know, $10 to $15 thousand a month to support your family and add that extra revenue to your business. So I don't need to say much more except with this cash out on the wings waiting to come back in, I think there is going to be an upward trend in the market place.

One more comment about the happenings of 1998: I think that we are going to look back on 1998 in the years to come and we will call it the correction of 1998. For anyone to call this a bear market, it would be quite a stretch. A bear market is described by a down-trending market of at least 20%. Did we technically have a dip of 20%? Yes we did. Has this been a down-trending year? Yes it has been, but if this is considered a "bear market", then you would have to call this the shortest bear market in the history. You would have to look back to 1990 and even coming out of the 1987 stock market crash when there were several dips to have any kind of comparison at all about how rapidly this market has recovered. So, a correction, even though it would be a big correction would be a little more than a 20% down turn. But I still think that is an appropriate word, and this correction now, you know, with bad news coming out of Asia and potentially South America and the news out of Russia, just had such a negative mental affect. About the only people that will call this last correction of '98 a bear market will be those that have newsletters to sell and put there neck on the line calling it a "bear market."

Now, specifically, we are going to look around this morning for things we can do on America Online (AOL) and Netscape (NSCP) and all that with the hype and the hoopla and the hysteria and all that on the Internet stocks. I am going to encourage my staff and myself even to be very careful with this. We can play the volatility of this marketplace, but remember, all and all over the long-term, good solid fundamentals backed up by technical analysis will always win out over rash decisions to jump in because it is going up. These Internet stocks are trading at such incredibly high multiples that they almost defy gravity. If not defying gravity, they surely defy the imagination that we as Americans are so gullible to buy stocks and to pay $400 and $500 for a batch of stocks that earn $1 in earnings, you know, that price earnings ratio on these things is so high that I am just going to caution everyone to be very careful, because if there is another is a downturn—another quick downturn or whatever—some of the profits, the value out of these high-multiple stocks is going to come out very quickly. Now having said that, it is probably going to run and run and run because there is so much sentiment for people getting involved in the Internet stocks, even though these companies are not making that much money compared to there stock prices. Everybody seems to want to be a player, and that's not just you and me, that's the big funds and a lot of the money. So they are going to be chasing after these stocks. I wouldn't be surprised to see a lot more stock splits in these Internet stocks like Amazon.com (AMZN) just did. I just think that it is a place to play it, as long as you understand the risk involved in playing high multiple stocks.

JANUARY 8, 1998
Good morning everyone, this is Wade!

With the big news of Alcoa Inc. (AA) announcing a stock split, a share buyback and an increase in the dividend and the stock not opening when I made a phone call a few minutes ago, I think it is going to create a lot of excitement in the whole market place because it is one of the DOW Jones 30's and I think it represents what is going to happen in the next few months.

I am scoping out the horizon, and there are just tons of stocks that are near their highs, they're making money, they're doing well and all nay-sayers and all the doom-sayers right now I think are just going to be put in their place here very quickly. I think we are going to see a nice robust economy, not as robust as it has been at times in the past, but very, very good from most standards. You know, that's our American economy. I think the worldwide economy is going to take a while to catch up.

I am looking at a bunch of stock splits coming up, and I think it is time to really have everyone study them out to see if there is a place where you want to get involved. Remember, there are five times to get involved. My favorite strategy is #4 where you get involved right when the stock is getting ready to split and it kind of rallies into the split date and the ex-dividend date and you get in for one or two days and then you are out. I think the second strategy, which is to get in on the announcement, is one of the toughest ones and I caution everyone because these stocks run up a little bit and they fall right back many times and a lot of people get burnt because the premiums for the options get so inflated upon the announcement that people will buy the higher premiums and then when the stock falls back a little bit, all of the air comes out of the premium and they end up losing. So be very, very careful on the announcement unless you can get in as a pre-announcement or right on the announcement. But anyway, I think there is going to be a lot of good stuff happening.

Right now I am in the middle of teaching a brand new Wall Street Workshop, getting ready to go into the studio and record it. We are on our second day right now. The class is doing very well. I made a special yesterday that I want to make for all of you. We have our newsletter which has a regular price of $139 a year. We have it on sale right now for $99, that's a one-year subscription.

JANUARY 11, 1998
Good morning everyone, this is Wade!

I was listening on the radio, and the market was expected to open up big one minute and the next minute it is going to be down. Yet there seems to be so much momentum with the DOW closing at an all time high of 9643 on Friday. You got to be saying "how am I going play this thing," and "how am I going to be playing individual stocks within this marketplace." We are obviously in the middle of a Bull Market spurt and it could continue to go up and it would take quite significant bad news (another huge banking crisis or an actual impeachment. I don't even know if that is 100% sure of driving the market down.) You know, the momentum players are playing as ecstatic as can be right now.

I just got off the phone with my stockbroker and I go over a mountain pass and I can't reach him for a few minutes until I come down the other side almost every morning, so while I was riding into the mountain pass, we were talking about Broadcast.com (BCST) that announces a 2:1 split. You really got to question how a whole bunch of people would go for some newsy type information that is coming out a day before and have the stock go up $90 in one day, yet here is a lot of momentum. It is just crazy that a company that does an I.P.O. six weeks ago can go that high not based on any kind of real earnings or anything else. Commenting on this with my stockbroker, here is another stock that is in La-La land, his statement was - and again this is not my statement, this is a statement of my stockbroker - "Ours is not to ask why, ours is to buy, buy, buy." Now I don't 100% buy into that, but this is kind of humorous and maybe it is good to start Monday on a humorous note. There are a bunch of these that are just running like crazy.

I just read an interesting article over the weekend out of the most recent edition of *Individual Investor* Magazine. Towards the back there was a man who had written—he was a stock player and I guess a fund manager or something, I can't remember—about asset allocation. It is at home right now, so if I get the page number and the edition, I will give it to you later. You know, you talk about asset allocation and about it is more important to have your money invested—and I think he was recommending 100% stocks right now—but it is more important to have your money allocated to the right types of investments,

according to your risk/reward portfolio ratio, than it is to choose a
particular fund manager or whatever. He was giving all kinds of comparisons about 90% of the gains is just by being in the market when the
market is going ahead. He was not that big into "market timing", he
kind of downplays "market timing". If you look at my books and seminars, you will never, ever hear me talking about "market timing". I
have never been a big believer in "market timing". It is better, if you are
going to play the stock market, to just buy and hold a particular stock
over the long-term, rather than try to buy and sell that stock according
to what you think the market is going to do. However, that is kind of
a stodgy old way of thinking and if you look at the Wade Cook strategy, you will find not doing "market timing" except for one particular
strategy like Range Riders or Reverse Range Rider where we might
buy options on a particular stock and they can hit the peak, or as they
bottom out we can ride it back up or ride it back down. So our type of
"market timing" is to turn the stock market into a business and buy
wholesale and sell retail, or sell retail and then buy back wholesale. It
is a whole different strategy compared to what the world teaches. Once
again, when you want the cutting edge strategies, you need to come to
a guy like Wade Cook and my seminars and my other instructors and
their courses like our SUPPORT Seminars. If you don't have information on the SUPPORT Seminars, you ought to call our 800 number
and get it–1-800-872-7411–and ask about the six different SUPPORT
Seminars we have going on around the country. They are really quite
remarkable and they have all been now adjusted to handle beginning
stock market players. Originally when we came up with our SUP-
PORT Seminars, they were designed to handle people who had already been through the Wall Street Workshop™, but now the first 45
minutes to 1 hour of each class is for beginners, to get them up to
speed. Again, the whole idea of turning the stock market into a business is to use it to generate cash flow. This strategy I don't think any
major fund managers with the old stodgy way of thinking on Wall
Street will ever come up to speed, because they just don't get it. They
don't understand people who have $2,000 or $3,000 to invest, or more
–want to use $2,000 or $3,000 as their risk money–and use that money
to generate income so they can buy other investments. They always

pretend like everyone in the whole market place has millions of dollars like they do, and they don't understand the little guys out here who are just trying to make money to pay their bills or give more money to their church.

So anyway, back to momentum investing: I think that there is a lot of money to make in the next while in momentum investing to just grab some stock or some options and latch on to them. I don't think it appropriate to, according to your stockbroker and your making a decision on how much money you want to put up a risk, and remember it is a risk, but again, where else but with options, for example on Internet stocks, do you get to buy an option on an America Online (AOL) or whatever, and get all the upside potential with only your option money as downside risk. It really is quite an interesting ratio where option money really becomes safety money where you can play in any rally or downturn with option money, which is a small proxy type of leveraged investment to get maximum return. So again, when you are thinking of safety first and you want safety in your investments, you need to come to Stock Market Institute of Learning, Inc.™ for that and not rely on the old way of thinking because it seems like that way of thinking just gets a lot of investors in trouble. So safety first, safety first, safety first and then cash flow, cash flow, cash flow.

JANUARY 25, 1998
Good morning, this is Wade.

I guess by now all the people with IQ Pager™ have the announcement that Microsoft (MSFT) has announced a 2:1 split. They made the announcement at 5:18 PST. I commend our Trading Department once again for looking at the past history and astorcating that it was going to make a stock split announcement today or next Monday. (Note: For information on IQPager™, call 1-800-872-7411.)

I had just a few reservations. I was telling everyone last week in California that Microsoft would probably make the announcement and it would be very exciting. I was talking to people about it, and the only reservation I had was that they are in the middle of the government lawsuit. But then I started thinking over the weekend, you know, if Microsoft makes a stock split announcement, they will be doing exactly what they have been doing, they will be staying true to form, and basically they will be saying to the government "We are not guilty of anything, knock off the nonsense!"

I once again commend all of our W.I.N.™ subscribers to one of the December issues of National Review magazine. On the cover it says "The Absurd Case Against Microsoft" It is a great article, a I ask you all to read it, and as a matter of fact, I will try to get permission from the magazine to post the article on W.I.N.™ so you could read the whole thing right here in its entirety. Right now, you would have to go out and scout around to try and find that. I think it was the first issue in December.

But anyway, it's a 2 for 1, it is an exciting day. I would not be surprised to see International Business Machines (IBM) to follow up with a stock split announcement, I'd be looking for Intel (INTC), and Dell (DELL), and a lot of the other computers to do the same thing. As you know, Sun Microsystems (SUNW) did one last week. A lot of these companies (not all) run in groups, a whole sector of the economy will get up to a certain high with their stock prices, and then within a few days or weeks will begin to make stock split announcements.

There will be a lot of excitement on Microsoft today. We loaded up last week on a bunch of short-term options, we will probably be selling them later, or watching them very closely for a run-up in the stock price. Already in after hours trading, it went from $155 up to around $160, and may even go a bit higher. Remember, there are many times to play these, so just keep watching it. Pick the best one for you, between you and your stockbroker according to your risk tolerance level. I wish you well!

MARCH 22, 1999

Good morning, this is Wade.

This is an interesting day of playing basketball, but a more interesting day once I got back in the car.

An unusual thing happened with expiration date on Friday. This is the first day, Monday, after the expiration date for March 1999. FDX Corporation (FDX) had announced a 2:1 stock split a few days before expiration, and we had put in place 40 contracts of the $90/$95 Bull Put Spread. In doing a Bull Put Spread, we are hoping to make a certain amount of money based on a net credit, or money that we make by selling the $95 puts and buying the $90 puts in this example. We made $\frac{1}{2}$ in this $5 spread, which means that we had $18,000 on hold or tied up in margin in our account to make $2,000. And it was just a three-day play, so that in of itself is a nice return.

Here is the unusual thing that happened. The stock today opened up at 96\frac{1}{4}$, and shortly after the open, we found out that we had 1,000 shares of the stock put to us at the $95 price. Since we had 40 contracts, we could have had up to 4,000 shares put to us, but the computer only assigned us 1,000. Remember, in a spread position, you still have an obligation in a Bull Call Spread, you would have an obligation on the upper strike price call that you sold, in a Bull Put Spread, you have an obligation to have put to you the stock at a certain strike price if the stock is below the strike price. Or so one would think. In this case here, the stock was above the $95 strike price, so in theory, there is no way that this stock should have gotten put to us. But it did.

Now, a few thoughts. If the stock is at or near the strike price, there is always a chance of getting called out on a Covered Call basis, or having the stock put to you on a short put position. However, once again, this stock was really not that close, in that it was at $96 at the close on Friday, and opened up at 96\frac{1}{4}$ on the open on Monday. What we did, was immediately sell the stock for 96\frac{1}{4}$, which means on the 1,000 shares we made an extra 1\frac{1}{4}$, or $1,250 less transaction costs on selling the stock that we purchased this morning on having it put to us.

If you would like more information on the Wealth Information Network™, visit us at www.wadecook.com, or call 1-800-872-7411.

2

INSANITY

Buy low, sell high. Buy wholesale, sell retail. Buy on weakness, sell on strength. Buy the stock on weakness, sell the call on strength.

—WADE B. COOK

T he following is taken from a recent letter sent to the graduates of our seminars. Although the content was originally designed to sell the most dynamic and value packed special Wade has ever offered, I found the product descriptions so informative that I chose to include it here.

Prices have been omitted. If you desire pricing or other information, simply call 1-888-WADECOOK.

Dear Wall Street Workshop Graduate or Wealth U Student:
Insanity doesn't strike Wade very often, but when it does it hits hard. Recently he was in our nation's capital, Washington D.C., speaking at the Semper Financial™ Regional Investors Educational Convention. If you haven't been to one of these conventions you should really get there.

The second day of the convention Wade was walking back to the hotel. This is in 102° heat and 92% humidity, so maybe that's the reason he went a little crazy. He was thinking about the 700 plus students who flew in from all over the country. He wanted to give them something special for persevering to get their education and be really successful. He wanted to show his gratitude for their support during a most interesting experience with ABC's *Good Morning America* during the event. He wanted something so spectacular that everyone would want to participate. So in his closing address, Wade put together on the spur of the moment the most incredibly valuable package he's ever offered.

This is what Wade told us when he came back: "I felt deeply for these people; some were beginners, some more advanced in their trading, and others needing more technical help. So obviously I thought: sell them something. People always feel better when they buy something. And what I sell is knowledge, knowledge that keeps on producing cash flow. Samuel Johnson said, *'Knowledge always desires increase; it is like fire, which must be kindled by some external agent, but which will afterward propagate itself.'* That's what I do, I kindle and feed the flame of knowledge about cash flow."

"My brain went to work devising a plan. You see, what I came up with was in the $7,000 to $10,000 package range. It was a collection of home study—audio and video courses which would truly help people make better trades and therefore make more money."

"But then the pricing, you know, the value for each dollar spent had to be incredible, a super good deal. I say incredible and I wanted to even redefine the word for this special. So here I am, out walking, thinking of a package or grouping of home study courses which will make a genuine impact in our students' lives—an impact of more cash flow, more consistent returns, fewer mistakes. *In short I wanted to put together an irresistible package.*"

And that's just what he did! This is a bare-bones, no-frills letter, not a glossy brochure, first because we wanted to get it to you as quickly as possible so you can get started adding to your trading success, and second because we are putting all that savings into this incredible package.

First let me ask you: How do you learn best? From a live person who has done what they are teaching, right? That's why our live, experiential workshop style is so successful. But what happens when you go home? How do you review? Notes are good, manuals and reading materials are good, but it's been proven that the more senses you learn with, the more successful you'll be.

That's why we develop video versions of our most important courses. Here are some of the benefits you get from owning courses on video:

- You get seminars personally tailored to fit your time and schedule. With videos, you can literally design your own workshop, picking and choosing what strategies to focus on. Review as much or as little as you choose, whenever you can!

- You get the visual dimension. See the charts being explained, follow along with the examples, and get the facilitator's full instruction. Using sight and hearing at the same time increases attention and comprehension, and that leads to more successful trades! Most of our courses have blank manuals for your notes plus a filled-in version.

- You get instant replay! If you miss something, run the tape back and watch the example again. Stop the tape, try it out, come back and review immediately to see the right result. You can go over a concept or strategy as many times as it takes to really be comfortable with it.

- Share the education with your friends and loved ones, *for no additional charge.* You can take just one volume or the whole course anywhere you want to watch it. Only video provides every chart, strategy, tip and technique as you learned them (except for the live experience). If you can't get folks to the Workshops, take the Workshops to them!

• Video copies of Stock Market Institute of Learning's™ workshops are like getting free college courses forever when you pay for just one semester! Every time you review a strategy you learn something new. Our most successful students attend courses every month. Having your own video copy essentially allows you to attend as often as you want at your own convenience.

• You can review on demand. Did you ever have a trade go wrong and wonder what happened? Would you like to have a mentor on hand any time of the day or night to go over the strategy with you? That's what video makes available—the opportunity for immediate course correction any time you get off track, for years to come.

• The handsome multi-volume reference libraries keep you in action toward your goals. Just by sitting on the shelf, our video sets remind you of what you could be doing with your time and money to achieve your dreams. And you'll be able to act on them, whether you want early retirement, freedom from debt or simply a better lifestyle for your family.

Now, let me tell you about what Wade called his "Good Morning, America" Special from the Washington D.C. Semper Financial Convention. We're calling it his Temporary Insanity Special—wait until you see this package! This are two *major* products, plus two other courses Wade ended up throwing in as a bonus, plus several other items that take this offer way past spectacular. Right up front you can see that any one of these is worth the whole price of the special, but we'll get into that later.

NEW WALL STREET WORKSHOP VIDEO™ SET

In the Wall Street Workshop™ every minute is so packed with explosive, practical information that going through it once is not enough. Now you can study these cutting-edge cash flow strategies with this 10-volume New Wall Street Workshop Video set. This is a reminder to retake the course live as well, because as of April of 1999 it is all new, updated for the new millennium!

Regular review of the thirteen basic formulas can mean extra money in your pocket *now*. Use that cash flow to pay off debt (or just pay the bills!), buy the house or car you've been wanting, spend more time with family, or build assets toward a great retirement. You know what your dream is—go for it!

This awesome home-study package features:

- Two full days of training in ten power-packed volumes. That is around *16 hours* of complete education, including an Early Bird Session where students research and practice the deals right in class.

- A course workbook with space for notes, plus a filled-in version so you can check your answers.

- Powerful and simple stock market strategies that novice and experienced investors alike can apply for immediate income potential.

- The ultimate teacher of Wade Cook strategies, Wade Cook himself! As the busy CEO of a multi-million dollar company, Wade rarely teaches the Wall Street Workshop live these days. Video is your best chance to get this fundamental knowledge direct from the source!

Even if you didn't know the first thing about trading, you will finish with more knowledge than many professionals have. Before getting into the strategies Wade starts with ground rules for getting the most out of your Workshop experience:

- How to apply and master the formulas through Simutrading™ without risking a penny—Study, Practice, Understand, then Do.

- How to know when you are ready to put real money into the market

.• What sources to turn to for information and advice.

Then we get into the meat: the strategies that can let you achieve a lifestyle beyond your dreams!

STRATEGY ONE: BUILDING A GREAT PORTFOLIO

Dive right into the nuts and bolts of stock market investing, broken down into manageable chunks.

- How stock price fluctuates with supply and demand.

- Measuring company strength through fundamental analysis.

- How to determine entry and exit points with technical analysis.

- Other factors that can influence stock price and movement.

- Who the players are: market makers, specialists and brokers.

- How to find a good personal broker.

- The difference between full service, discount, deep discount and online brokers.

STRATEGY TWO: ROLLING STOCK

One of the easiest ways to get cash flowing your way is Rolling Stocks. Rolling stocks move up and down in price in a consistent, recognizable pattern. By identifying the stock's trading range, you can buy near the bottom and sell near the top, and repeat.

- Definition of rolling stock, support and resistance.

- How to determine the trading range.

- Three rules of playing rolling stocks successfully.

- Three roll patterns you can recognize to make better trades.

STRATEGY THREE: OPTIONS

Options are risky, but Wade's formulas let you manage and minimize risk *and* make more money. With an option, you are exchanging money for the right or the obligation to buy or sell stock at a specific price on or before an established expiration date. The leverage you get from options provides phenomenal returns. You'll understand how it can be worth the risk!

- Options vocabulary

- The benefits of playing options

- Identifying stocks poised to move

- How to avoid losses

- Stocks vs. options—ways to get less risk out of options

- The power of LEAPS®

STRATEGY FOUR: STOCK SPLITS

Some companies regularly add to the amount of their shares available in the market, reducing the price of the stock by the same factor. A company announcing a 2 for 1 split will double the number of shares, making the stock half the pre-split price. Historically, strong stocks that split tend to grow back to their pre-split levels within two years or so, and options leverage multiplies your profits!

- Why companies do stock splits

- Where to find splitting companies

- How playing options on stock splits increases profit potential

- The five basic times to get involved in a stock split play

- How to determine which options to buy

- When to exit the trade, placing sell orders when you buy

- Cautions for Split Strategy #2

- New insights on Split Strategy #4, rallying into the split

New: Extra profits (and loss avoidance) on Split Strategy #4B or pre-#5–the dip on the split date or shortly after the ex-dividend date (*Note:* Wade says this strategy alone is worth the cost of the whole package!)

STRATEGY FIVE: WRITING COVERED CALLS

If you already own stock you can generate monthly cash flow by writing covered calls, a strategy you can even do in an IRA. Each month you sell someone the right, in the form of a call option, to buy your stock at a price you're happy with. If the stock rises above that "strike price," your stock will be bought, or "called away" from you, and you get the profit. If the stock ends up below the strike price, you keep the stock and can sell calls again next month. Either way, you pocket the premium from selling the call.

- Definition of a covered call

- The covered call formula (three steps)

- How to calculate yields

- Five power strategies (two are new!)

- What to do if the stock goes down

- When to expect getting called out.

Note: There are even more new Covered Call strategies in Wade's *newest* course, Red Light, Green Light (keep reading for more information)!

STRATEGY SIX: SELLING PUTS (WADE'S FAVORITE FORMULA)

Selling puts generates amazing profit for those with the necessary cash and approvals. Selling brings in cash, so why not sell someone the right to sell you stock, called a put option, at a price you are willing to pay. If the option is exercised, you get stock that you already decided you wanted to own at a wholesale price! And if the option expires, you keep the premium for selling, just as in covered calls.

- Two rules of selling puts

- How to buy stocks at wholesale

- What to do if you have stock put to you, or how to avoid it with roll-outs

- Margin requirements for selling puts (all *new*, very valuable information!)

- When to buy back and free up margin

- Why you should get better at selling than buying

- Advanced strategies: tandem plays and spreads–the awesome Bull Put Spread

- Bull Call Spreads: definitions and examples

- What to watch out for in Debit Spreads

STRATEGY SEVEN: PEAKS AND SLAMS

The last of the seven main strategies uses stocks that have seen a dramatic price change within a day or two. Stocks may rise sharply or fall heavily due to news or the whims of the market. Since the stock often retraces much of that movement within a similar time frame of a day or so, we can use that tendency to profit from the recovery.

- Definition of peaks and slams

- How to find favorable candidates

- When to get in and out

- Play the news–reversals

MID-TERM STRATEGIES

Strategies Eight through Eleven focus on longer-term bargain-hunting. You want to find companies with promise and buy their stock while it's still cheap. When others start to catch on, you ride the wave up. These are ways to identify good bargain prospects and put yourself in a position to profit.

- Strategy Eight: IPOs 25 day rule

- Strategy Nine: Turnarounds

- Strategy Ten: Spin-Offs

- Strategy Eleven: Penny Stocks

COMBINING STRATEGIES

These strategies tweak the basics of Rolling Stock to broaden profit possibility. Range Riders roll in a definable range that trends upwards or downwards rather than sideways. Rolling Options takes the leverage of buying and selling options to let you "roll" stocks in higher price ranges. If a stock rolls between $95 and $99, buying and selling the stock only brings you a 5% return with each cycle. An option on that stock, however, might trade for around $10 at the lower range. If it goes up to $12.50 or $13 as the stock reaches $99, that's a 25 or 30% return!

- Strategy Twelve: Range Riders

- Strategy Thirteen: Rolling Options

With all these great strategies, you will have more than enough to get your money working overtime so you don't have to. We wrap things up with a discussion of how to build and balance a great blue chip portfolio.

- The three stages of wealth.

- Choosing the right strategies for you.

- Balancing your portfolio of strategies.

- Creating a plan just for you.

Studying the Wall Street Workshop Video™ will put you well on the way to achieving your freedom. That doesn't mean that there is nothing more to learn, however. Consistent review and practice of these basic strategies has allowed our students to improve the lives of their families, build up their communities, and fulfill their own dreams. Let me share with you a recent note we received:

We made $230,079 today, January 12, 1999, on CMGI–a Tech stock. In fact, on January 11 we made $47,855, and on January 7 we made $46,644. We've made $372,725 in just the opening days of this month...we've never lost a dime when we *followed the rules as taught at the Wall Street Worskhop™.*

> *A year ago today we were living on 20 plus credit cards and had a second loan out on our home. Today we're down to 2 or 3 credit cards and that second loan has been paid off. And we don't owe much on the cards. A year ago we didn't know if we were going to keep this damn house. Now it's paid for. All due to the lessons we learned at [Stock Market Institute of Learning, Inc.]!*
>
> —JOEL & JENNIFER D., CA

That's just one small example of what you can accomplish when you take advantage of this special package. This course tuition is the same as our bottom-most drop-down price for the live Wall Street Workshop: $4,295. The video set by itself is on sale right now for $2,995. This is one part of the package... read on.

NEW NEXT STEP VIDEO™ SET

Continuing *quality* education is the key to success, and Wade Cook Seminars is dedicated to making that education available to you in the most convenient format.

We thought the best thing to explain the Next Step™ Seminar to you is letting the attendees speak:

> *This was absolutely the best seminar to date–can't wait to implement everything I have learned! This seminar will enhance my skills 100 fold! Thank you!!*
>
> —SCOTT S., NV

> *The tips and techniques in charting such as trendlines, how and where to draw them as well as the instruction on Telechart 2000® was of particular interest as it allowed me to set up my Telechart to get out of it more of what it is capable of.*
>
> *This seminar should reduce my risk as well as help me to be*

much more selective in the trades I will make. Most importantly, those trades will be more profitable.

—EDWIN K., WI

Learning how to load and use the 'hot keys' setting on my computer which if I would have known three weeks ago would have cut my losses to $3,000 or $4,000 and not the $16,300 I lost! After the first day I know enough to go back and see what I did wrong. I couldn't afford not to come...

—GARY F., CA

I loved the sections on charting, recognizing trends and identifying support and resistance. I feel like we have been trading blindly without these tools. Candlesticks were also very interesting and I'm anxious to learn more.

I feel ready to really make some money now in a careful and systematic process.

—ANDREA C., OR

But our favorite comment about the Next Step Seminar came from an attendee in Florida:

This class should be mandatory within 90 days after the Wall Street Workshop! It is so informative that it would have increased my portfolio 100% within those 90 days just knowing when to get out of a trade based on the charts!

—SHARON M., FL

We couldn't put it any better. However well you are doing in the market, the longer you trade without taking the Next Step the more money it will cost you in your trading results. If you are using any of the Wall Street Workshop strategies you *need* this education in your trading library. Here is an overview of this course you can take at your leisure in your home or office:

- Like the Wall Street Workshop Video set, the Next Step™ Videos include everything in the live course–sixteen hours in nine volumes, including the Early Bird trading sessions.

- Workbooks from the live courses, one copy with blanks for your notes and the other filled in for your reference.

- Twelve topics covered in depth–technical analysis training that will let you multiply your returns and dramatically cut losses while you trade the basic Wall Street Workshop strategies, plus advanced strategies including Puts, Spreads and Combos.

- Featuring Keven Hart, Ryan Litchfield and Paul Cook, experts in technical analysis and three of the best teachers we have ever had the pleasure to work with. One recent Next Step student put it this way:

Keven Hart is one of my favorite instructors; he makes it all very easy to understand. And Ryan Litchfield is so intense! The things he taught are incredible–he's got so much information and relays it so well! It takes a lot of concentration, but we learned so much. I can't say enough good about him!

—WARD O., NV

CHARTING: THE EDGE OF THE ROAD

Ryan and Keven start out with the most fundamental of technical analysis, charting. Charts are available in many time periods: daily, weekly, monthly, yearly, and even minutes on intra-day charts. The time period of your charts is important–it should match the time frame of the strategy you are using. If you are playing a Stock Split Entry #2, the announcement, and hoping to get in and out in a few hours or minutes, you need an intra-day chart to recognize the best exit signals. How the stock has been doing over the past five years is not going to be useful!

- Bar charts

- Time periods

- The direction of price movements

- The Great Leap

- Recognizing breakouts

- Uptrends and downtrends

PRICE LEVEL SUPPORT/RESISTANCE: ROAD BLOCKS
Technical analysis is an illustration of the psychology of the market at work. Charts are a visual demonstration of what investors are thinking.

- Historic Levels

- Support and Resistance

- Outriders

- The Chumps and Suckers Syndrome

RETRACEMENT: DETOURS
When a stock or index has run up steeply there is a tendency for it to "take a breather" and retrace some of the gain. Knowing about retracement can help you tell whether a reversal is long-term or whether the stock is readying itself for another climb.

- What the percent of retracement shows

- Short term vs. Long Term retracements

- How to use retracements to recognize and buy on dips

GAPS: THE END OF THE ROAD

When a stock opens and the price is higher than the previous day's high or lower that the previous day's low, we call it a "gap." You can literally see a gap on the chart. When this happens on increased volume, it can be a very valuable indicator of trend continuation or of a major reversal. Gaps are a powerful tool for making sure you ride *with* the momentum instead of battling the tide while your capital is washed away!

- Definition of a chart gap

- Continuation gaps

- Gaps to ignore

- Warning gaps

- Body gaps

SIGNATURE MOVEMENTS: UNDER CONSTRUCTION

Signature movements are charts that show a dramatic change in the works. When you see one of these patterns forming, keep a close watch for profits ahead!

- Flags, flutters and pennants

- Stairs–the up-sideways-up movement

- Wedges–ascending, descending and equilateral

- Roman Candles

- The Kiss Goodbye

- Multiple Tops or Bottoms

CANDLESTICK CHARTING: INTERSECTIONS

Candlestick charts focus on price momentum, a powerful way to define entry and exit points. Candlesticks help identify tops and bottoms. With about three days to confirm a movement, you can use these charts to really get ahead of the market in many cases.

- Trading Momentum

- Japanese Candlesticks

- Displays of Emotion

- Covered Calls

- DUCks and DUC/Cs

- Overbought conditions

- Market movement

- Dojis–the exception to the rule

- Reversal and Continuation Candlestick Patterns

OEX: TRADING THE MARKET

The OEX is the index of the S&P 100 stocks, and there are options on the index itself, allowing you to play movements in the market as a whole without having to identify which particular stocks are heading up or down. The OEX is extremely volatile and can move quickly, making it one of the most popular day trading strategies.

- Types of indexes

- Settlement

- Characteristics of the OEX

- Using the OEX

- Naked positions

- Cash flow with OEX options

- Charting to identify trends

- Protecting portfolios with OEX options

The outline above is just Day One of the *new* Next Step! The information you obtain from these videos will dramatically expand your financial horizons. By the time you finish watching even one video, you'll be too excited to even sleep! You will learn how to ride the market up, down, and all around, and make money consistently. You will hear how you can limit your risk and harness maximum profits in trade after trade.

> *Learning not to be afraid of the market or alarmed by what it does is invaluable. There are ways to make money in each and every market...Keven Hart and Ryan Litchfield are the most outstanding instructors I have encountered in over fifty years.*
> —PETER M., IL

This Next Step Video package taught by Wade Cook, Keven Hart, Ryan Litchfield and Paul Cook is very dynamic—it will knock your socks off!

NEW RED LIGHT, GREEN LIGHT™ AUDIO COURSE

Wade Cook just completed one of the most successful home/car study courses ever. This is the ultimate course on making timely trades. (Just a note here—while some of our courses are still on cassette, we are taking everything to CD, and "Red Light, Green Light" is part of that process.)

Wade is the CEO of a publicly traded company and as such he has restrictions on what he can and cannot say or do during certain times of every quarter, then again at year end. He thought that, because other CEOs, CFOs, board members and other insiders would be under the same "news-no news" constrictions, and since most companies file their reports about the same time, that many stocks would behave (up or down) according to certain patterns.

Now, if you're playing options, those movements or lack thereof could have dramatic effects on your profitability. So Wade went into the studio, and in front of students, and he wrote extensively on this timing phenomenon. This course will take you from the beginning and show you how to make better trades and how to avoid lousy trades.

Here's what the course includes:

- Two plus hours of video education with Wade himself teaching his new discovery of the quarterly "news/no news" pattern, using charts and overheads to show you examples of how this pattern has played out in recent years. Two videos are included: the "Red Light, Green Light" basic course and a second class on using the formulas for cash flow with the help of the "news/no news" format.

- Audio–nine compact discs with nearly nine hours of education

- Manuals, Special Reports and Articles: Jam-packed information in writing with many charts and examples to explore the process and use this information to immediately make a difference in your trading style.

- Transparencies for each of the 12 months to configure with TC2000®. Print out any company's chart, place it behind the transparency and see the patterns. Each company is different (ending periods for the quarters, type of news and filing dates).

- Explanation enough on all these points to help you see how this process works.

- Identifying the "red light" intervals that point to the successful turnaround months.

- Understanding the stringent guidelines the SEC places on Boards of Directors, Company Presidents, CFOs and CEOs, and how those rules affect stock price.

- How quarterly reporting dates affect the "green light" intervals.

- Planning vacations during the "red light" intervals when the market dies, or do puts and Bear Call Spreads.

- The most important question you can ask in your trade analysis: What compelling reason does this stock or option have to go up?

- Comparing 40 years of market performance (this will astound you!)

- Buy on rumors, sell on fact/news—the impact of anticipated events.

- Getting good with your pick of five companies using "Red Light, Green Light" strategies.

- Major Board of Directors decisions and how they affect your timing getting into a trade.

- Profit-taking in "green light" intervals.

- You will learn why *not* to buy call options in the first two weeks of February, May, August and December!

- What "green light" intervals and rallies have in common.

- What the "January effect" is and how to profit from it.

- Erratic "red light" months, and what to do about them.

- Knowing when to sell before the "red light" intervals.

- How to generate cash flow whether the light is red or green.

- Choosing the right moment to get involved (or uninvolved) for profit taking.

- Information gathering processes–mergers, acquisitions, stock splits, earnings, IPOs.

- The working rules; making it fun and profitable.

HULA MOOLA™–WADE COOK LIVE

Now, before we go on we must bring up an awesome event. In June Wade taught the first Hula Moola in Honolulu, Hawaii. He loved it, and so did the students! The format was designed so people could take their families and have a lot of free time. The class was five days –Monday through Friday, from 7:00 to 10:00 A.M. In Hawaii the stock market opens at 3:30 A.M. Some students got up then and their day was in full swing when they came to class at 7:00 A.M. There was basically one topic–whatever was important to Wade to talk about that day. You know we were ready to have a blast! They discussed the Red Light, Green Light process, spreads like Bull Put Spreads and Bear Call Spreads, stock splits (a lot of this!) and too many other topics to list here.

Read the comments of people who attended:

Hula Moola was Great! I really learned a lot while having a great time in Hawaii. Let's do more!

–ROBERT N., CA

This week has been inspirational, instructional and fun. The fast pace challenges us to stay focused. Your family/staff are wonderful. You have encouraged us in the market and inspired us in our spiritual and personal lives..

—BUD & NANCY S., OK

Wade is a great instructor and when he is done explaining something I do understand it. During this seminar I made about $19,000 during the week on information that was provided.

—BERRY S., WI

This was the best seminar yet. To be able to hear from you [Wade] and also still be able to have time to do things with my family. The class is wonderful and has changed my life completely. I am becoming debt free and sponsoring a missionary which has been my goal.

—CHARLIE C., TX

We brought our 12-year-old son along and turned this into a family vacation, so we really liked having an early morning brief class 7-10 AM for five days. It was definitely a plus to have this class run in a location where with the time zone change the stock market closed in the morning. This then kept us on track for a vacation rather than watching the stock market all day.

—SUZANNE W., IL

This is great. I like the layout—you can combine learning and vacation. I would like to do this again.

—ALFA & TONY G., WA

Thank you so much for sharing all the information you did with this Hula Moola. I loved the scheduling, topics, etc. I would have been happy even if the classes were six hours a day. I feel more clear about the direction I need to go and how to cut losses more effectively and wind out of positions. I especially love the time we spent on Bull Put and Bear Call Spreads with the wind-out thoughts and scenarios. Thanks again!

–JIM D., HI

SPREAD & BUTTER™ VIDEO COURSE

And believe it or not, it gets still better for you. (We were checking Wade's temperature at this point!) Wade also threw in, as a bonus, his wildly imaginative Spread & Butter™ One-Day Video Seminar. This new home study course is a live taping of Wade himself teaching his great cash flow spread strategies. Here are examples of the teaching from this valuable course:

Sometimes unfamiliar stock market vocabulary keeps us from researching and investing in the market. The term "spreads" could be one of those. Without full knowledge, it could mean anything from a spread on a bet to the spread on top of toast. In the stock market a "spread" is used to limit the downside on a trade, set up when you buy an option and sell an option on the same stock.

The four types of spreads are insurance or "hedge" strategies that "billion dollar" types use to protect their deals, but the little guy can use them just as well. Spreads can be used in up markets (Bull Call Spreads and Bull Put Spreads) and down markets (Bear Call Spreads and Bear Put Spreads).

In a Bull Call Spread we would purchase and own an $85 call option and sell the $90 call option, thus creating a $5 "spread." Buying 10 contracts this would create a $5,000 profit minus the "net debit" – what we paid for the $85 call minus what we took in by selling the $90 call. So if setting up this spread cost us $3,700, our profit would be $1,300 ($5,000 minus the $3,700 net debit). For Bull Call Spreads we want the stock to close above the higher strike price so we purchase the stock for $85 (substituted with options) and are called out at $90 and pocket that $1,300.

A Bull Put Spread is commonly called a Put Credit Spread. In a case where we'd do a Bull Put Spread on a stock priced at $87, we would buy an $80 put and sell an $85 put. Notice that both of these strike prices are slightly out of the money. The premium we would get paid on the $85 put will be more than the price we pay for the $80 put. The difference is where we earn the credit. The objective is to have the stock be above the $85 strike price at expiration so that both options expire and we keep the credit.

Wade also educates you on how Index Spreads and Calendar Spreads can be used effectively. Buying slightly in the money and following other rules you will learn, these valuable tools can fit nicely in your investment toolbox.

With Spreads you can figure out your risk and profits in advance. Spreads are set up to provide steady income now! Spreads are a strategy you can start using with fairly small amounts of cash, and your brokers will love it (once they learn it!).

You will learn in this seminar how $25,000 can generate $10,000 to $12,000 per month, even if you have one trade out of four or five go bad! Check the video course for details. A few more points you will learn from Spread & Butter™ Home Study Course:

- Spreads are an easy tool for generating income.

- The four types of spreads: two credit spreads and two debit spreads. Use credit spreads to save on commissions.

- Specific spread time periods to make more money and avoid losses.

- The obligations you are under when you set up a spread by selling a call or put.

- Spreads let you limit your downside risk and your margin requirements.

- The upside of spreads is also limited, but good—25 to 40% monthly returns are possible with Bull Put Spreads and Bear Call Spreads.

- How newer traders without huge portfolios can use spreads.

- Variations on spreads for different situations.

- Spread combinations as stocks or options move up and down.

- A new formula for the brain—Sell first!

- Spreads, like Covered Calls, are done monthly for real cash flow.

- Spreads present different risks than other cash-flow strategies. Diversify, diversify, diversify, even in risks!

- This seminar gives different ways to keep you in control of your monthly cash flow.

- Diversification is available by trading different trusts – SPY, MDY and SPDRS.

- If the rules are followed and spreads are done correctly, $25,000 can produce $10,000 plus of profit month after month.

FORTIFY YOUR INCOME™ VIDEO SET

We begged Wade to stop there. After all, you are already getting the Wall Street Workshop Video Set, the Next Step Video Set, Red Light, Green Light Audio course, AND his incredible Spread & Butter One-Day Seminar Videos, PLUS Wade himself *live* in Hawaii at the Hula Moola! That's a *complete cash-flow education*—education you can review as many times as you want, share with your spouse and family members, and use to fine tune your efforts, for years to come—for less than the bottom price of the Wall Street Workshop™ alone! If you still haven't called for this deal, maybe we need to check *your* temperature!

Amazingly, though, Wade still wouldn't stop! For the same price he threw in the Wall Street Workshop™ follow-up half-day seminar, Fortify Your Income™ (F.Y.I.™). This four-video set is great for reviewing the Wall Street Workshop strategies from a different angle, getting your cash flow turned on, and really keeping your trading on track. Let's go over the course agenda:

VOLUME 1: FINE TUNING

Do you practice your game every day? FYI will teach you how to do "lay ups" for your stock market business and inspire you to practice the basics of investing. You could be the Michael Jordan of stock market trading! Learn why it is vital to discover and develop your own personal style of trading, and gain skills in doing it.

Learn how to avoid most losses. We'll cover in depth the five things people do that lose money, so you can avoid them. Here they are in a nutshell (see, even here Wade insists on giving away the store!):

1. Investing all your risk capital at once. Instead you should:

    •   Paper trade until you are winning more than you lose, and do several trades.

    •   Learn how to hold on to your capital. The skills needed to keep money are different than those for making money. FYI teaches you ways to keep your money as well as make more.

    •   Treat the stock market as your business. Wade's definition of using the stock market as a business is "Buy something, sell something, and use the profit to pay the bills." This is such a foreign concept for most investors they often need to hear it more than once to understand how to put it in practice.

2. Not doing your homework.

    •   Many people don't effectively research the stocks they buy. Instead they buy because someone said it was a good deal, usually their broker or someone they work with. Wrong, wrong, wrong!

- Always check on the news about a company. Look at the charts and past earnings reports. Look at the people who are running the company. We'll review the proper research for good, solid trades and more money in your pocket!

3. Investing haphazardly and not using even dollar amounts.

- We often have several trades open at the same time. Here's the hazard—if you are not using even dollar amounts you can win more often than you lose and still lose overall.

4. Listening to the wrong people.

- Wade constantly asks to whom you are listening! Part of the learning process is being taught by someone who knows more than you. You can't learn from a person who knows less than you . The same goes for learning to make money.

- If you want to make $100,000 a year, then why are you listening to people, whether they be CPAs, brokers, attorneys or relatives, who are not making that much?

- If you want to be a millionaire, learn what millionaires do and copy it!

5. Trying to do too much at once.

- At the Wall Street Workshop we suggest you become an expert at one or two of the strategies. Experts focus on a specific talent, skill or profession until they are extraordinary.

- Pick one or two strategies, and focus on perfecting those until you are really good at it. Once you are an expert in that, you can pick and perfect another by practicing on paper until you are consistently making money—you'll already know what it's like to be an expert!

VOLUME 2: SPIN-OFF SURPRISES

Spin-offs and stock buybacks, along with stock splits, are among Wade's favorite strategies. Companies usually do stock buybacks when management believes the stock is undervalued–in other words, that it is trading at a bargain price. A buyback lets the company accomplish two things:

- Gain back additional control of the company by decreasing the percentage of stock owned by outsiders.

- Put more value in the stock, both by reducing the amount of shares in the "float" (the open market), and by increasing the perception of value. After all, who would know better than the company itself if the stock is a bargain

Make sure you do your research and homework on buybacks, however. Sometimes companies that are trading near or below their historical lows are actually seeing the effect of deeper problems. Watch the news and check the fundamentals to make sure a buyback company is still strong.

Spin-offs can also be terrific opportunities. When a company spins off part of its operation into a new company, the new company has several advantages:

- A proven product or service, plus an existing market in place.

- Experienced and motivated management.

- A parent company with a significant interest in the success of the spin-off, and often deep pockets to temporarily subsidize that success.

- More focus and agility to respond to market conditions.

Parent companies also gain from spinning off part of the operation–they often keep a controlling interest in the newer company, and at the same time reduce the amount of attention and investment they need to devote to that enterprise.

Just as with buybacks, do your homework and check news and fundamentals for each company to be sure the break-up is not due to or masking long-term troubles.

Volume 3: The Big Three and a New One

The "Big Three" of cash flow trading are ways to identify whether and when to get into and out of trades. Timing is everything, and we use the Big Three of fundamental analysis, technical analysis, and other motivating factors (OMFs) to decide *what to buy* (fundamentals), *when to buy* (technicals) and *why to buy now* (OMFs). This section of FYI teaches how to effectively use all three for your best trades.

Fundamentals

- P/E Ratio and what it tells you.

- Typical P/E ranges for the major exchanges.

- Earnings, growth, and stability indicators.

- What to look for in debt ratio and why it is important.

- How book value can tell you which stocks are a bargain.

- Yield, the buy-and-hold investor's bible.

Technical analysis

- The tools of technical analysis.

- Moving averages: what they are and how to use them.

- Momentum: catching the wave.

- Divergence/convergence: recognize probable stock moves before they happen.

- Volume contraction and expansion–tracking supply and demand.

- Call options vs. put options, and when to use each.

OTHER MOTIVATING FACTORS (OMFs)
- Newsy items

- Share Buybacks

- Mergers

- Lawsuits

- Spin-offs

- Bankruptcy

- Stock splits

- Earnings reports and pre-reports

THE NEW ONE: IPOs

IPOs, or Initial Public Offerings, are often out of reach for the individual investor, because the investment underwriters who manage the offering usually reserve huge blocks of shares for their best institutional and big-money customers. By the time the stock in the most attractive IPO companies hits the secondary market in the stock exchanges, the price has usually blown past its offering price, and it begins to drop down, sometimes taking weeks or months to approach that first-day frenzy price again.

But there are ways for you to play IPOs, using what Wade calls the 25-day wait. For 25 days after the initial offering the investment bank cannot make any public statements about the company; it's a type of quiet period. Just like in the Red Light, Green Light, quiet period *equals* no news *equals* no compelling reason for a stock to go up. Now, you might think of going to check some IPOs that came out in the first or early second quarter this year, and see what happens after the 25 day quiet period is over...

Also on Volume Three is a review of Options on Stock Splits. You know how big a piece of Wade's interest this strategy gets–you hear about it at almost every class, read about stock splits nearly every day on W.I.N.™ You can probably even repeat the five times to get involved with a stock split.

- Do you remember which ones are short-term plays and which are medium to longer-term? (Remember that Wade's definition of long-term is weeks or a few months, not years!)

- Do you remember when to take just a dollar or so in profit and get out, and which ones you can hang in for a potential double?

- Do you remember what technical indicators to look for in each phase before you get in?

This is the profit-making information FYI was designed to review and reinforce. It may not seem important to review what you think you already know, but where would Michael Jordan be if he quit practicing because he knew how to do a lay up.

- You need to be practicing this knowledge every day until it is second nature, and then keep practicing to keep it second nature. That's what millionaires and experts do!

VOLUME FOUR: COVERED CALLS TO SPREADS

Wade has always said he prefers to focus on the positive, and these strategies are based on finding stocks heading up. Bull Put and Bull Call Spreads have been explained in this letter under Wade's Spread & Butter Videos–FYI is one more chance to look at these powerful profit-enhancing and risk-limiting strategies. Every time you look at something like this you will learn more and more.

The second part of Volume Four is review of Covered Calls.

1. The three rules of Covered Calls:

   - Buy stock on margin.

   - Look for volatile stocks.

   - Use stocks in the $5 to $25 price range.

2. The two problems with Covered Calls:

   - You get called out of the best stocks and end up keeping the "dogs."

   - Stocks in the $5 to $20 price range may be less desirable and more risky than higher priced stocks.

The review of these basic strategies in FYI answers common questions we hear after the Wall Street Workshop, and will give you skills to solve problem trades you may be having.

VOLUME FIVE: MORE ON SELLING PUTS AND SPIDERS (SPDRs)

Volume Five starts with one of Wade's favorites, Selling Puts. Just like the Covered Call section, this will remind you of the rules of selling puts and address the common pitfalls new traders experience with this strategy. Selling puts is a tremendous strategy for putting money in your pocket immediately!

The FYI finishes up with another bonus strategy not covered in the Wall Street Workshop, SPIDERS–SPY, MDY and DIA. These are indexes you can trade like stocks, and take advantage of overall market movement without having to sort through all the stocks to find the right ones to play!

EVEN MORE BONUSES!!!

As if all that weren't enough, in D.C. Wade went on to include:

- Three *additional* months of W.I.N., added to whatever subscription you currently have.

- Three months of W.I.N. Plus, the e-mail stock split notification service, to save you having to check W.I.N. every few minutes for the latest on splits.

Then Wade stopped and looked at his Semper Financial enthusiasts–these people who had come from around the country and stayed through three days of heat, humidity and often overwhelming amounts of education–and he added one more bonus. He authorized attendance at an additional Semper Financial Convention for anyone who had paid to attend in D.C., and for anyone who signed up for Wall Street Workshop or Wealth U as a couple (they can have two free tickets)!

What if just one idea, one technique, one strategy in any one of these courses makes you $10,000? What if you use that strategy every month? No kidding, there are between 92 and 133 such strategies in this jumbo combo package, repeatable "meter drop" strategies. You need this information now–$10,000 times 12 months is $120,000 extra this year. There are millions of dollars of income just waiting for you. Do it now!

To your wealth!

3

AVAILABLE RESOURCES

T he following books, videos, and audiocassettes have been re-viewed by the Stock Market Institute of Learning, Inc.™, Light-house Publishing Group, Inc., or Gold Leaf Press staff and are suggested as reading and resource material for continuing education to help with your financial planning, and real estate and stock market trading. Because new ideas and techniques come along and laws change, we're always updating our catalog.

To order a copy of our current catalog, please write or call us at:

Stock Market Institute of Learning, Inc.™
14675 Interurban Avenue South
Seattle, Washington 98168-4664
1-800-872-7411

Or, visit us on our web sites at:
www.wadecook.com
www.lighthousebooks.com

Also, we would love to hear your comments on our products and services, as well as your testimonials on how these products have benefited you. We look forward to hearing from you!

AUDIOCASSETTES/CDS

13 FANTASTIC INCOME FORMULAS-A FREE COMPACT DISC
Presented by Wade B. Cook

Learn 13 cash flow formulas, some of which are taught in the Wall Street Workshop™. Learn to double some of your money in $2^1/_2$ to 4 months.

ZERO TO ZILLIONS™
Presented by Wade B. Cook

A four-album, 16-cassette, powerful audio workshop on Wall Street-understanding the stock market game, playing it successfully, and retiring rich. Learn 11 powerful investment strategies to avoid pitfalls and losses. Learn to catch "day-trippers," how to "bottom fish," write covered calls, and to possibly double your money in one week on options on stock split companies. Wade "Meter Drop" Cook can teach you how he makes fantastic annual returns in his account. You then will have the information to try to follow suit. Each album comes with a workbook, and the entire workshop includes a free bonus video called "Dynamic Dollars," 90 minutes of instruction on how all the strategies can be integrated, giving actual examples of what kinds of returns are possible so you can get in there and play the market successfully. A must for every savvy, would-be investor.

POWER OF NEVADA CORPORATIONS-A FREE CASSETTE
Presented by Wade B. Cook

Nevada Corporations have secrecy, privacy, minimal taxes, no reciprocity with the IRS, and protection for shareholders, officers, and directors. This is a powerful seminar.

INCOME STREAMS-A FREE CASSETTE
Presented by Wade B. Cook

Learn to buy and sell real estate the Wade Cook way. This informative cassette will instruct you in building and operating your own real estate money machine.

24 KARAT
Presented by Wade B. Cook

Learn how to protect your family's finances through anything–including Y2K! 24 Karat seminar on cassette teaches people how currency fluctuates and the safest currency to have. This seminar is packed with must-know information about your future.

THE FINANCIAL FORTRESS HOME STUDY COURSE
Presented by Wade B. Cook

This eight-part series is the last word in entity structuring. It goes far beyond mere financial planning or estate planning. It helps you structure your business and your affairs so that you can avoid the majority of taxes, retire rich, escape lawsuits, bequeath your assets to your heirs without government interference, and, in short-bomb proof your entire estate. There are six audiocassette seminars on tape, an entity structuring video, and a full kit of documents.

RED LIGHT,GREEN LIGHT™
Presented by Wade B. Cook

This is the ultimate on making timely trades. As CEO of a publicly traded company, Wade Cook discovered a quarterly pattern of stock price behavior that corresponds with corporate new reports. Since most companies file their reports about the same time, many stocks would move accordingly.

If you're playing options, those price movements–or lack thereof–have a dramatic effect on your returns. The Red Light,Green Light course shows you how to recognize and use this information to make more money and avoid losing trades. This "news-no news" discovery is exhilarating!

BOOKS

WALL STREET MONEY MACHINE, VOLUME 1
By Wade B. Cook

The revised and updated version of the book which appeared on the New York Times Business Best Sellers list for over one year, *Wall Street Money Machine, Volume 1* contains the best strategies for wealth enhancement and cash flow creation you'll find anywhere. Throughout this book, Wade Cook describes many of his favorite strategies for generating cash flow through the stock market: rolling stocks, proxy investing, covered calls, and many more. It's a great introduction for creating wealth using the Wade Cook formulas.

WALL STREET MONEY MACHINE, VOLUME 2: STOCK MARKET MIRACLES

Finally, a book by an author that understands what the average investor needs: knowing when to sell. The information in this book will give you the ability to make money using real tried-and-true techniques. No special knowledge required, no strings attached. These tools can help you secure real wealth. Thanks to Wade Cook, financial miracles happen every day for thousands of students who are applying what they learned from this book. Buy and read *Wall Street Money Machine, Volume 2: Stock Market Miracles* today and see what happens in your life.

WALL STREET MONEY MACHINE, VOLUME 4: SAFETY 1ST INVESTING
By Wade B. Cook

Over two decades of research and experience have culminated in Wade Cook's book, *Safety 1st Investing*. In it you will learn how to "preserve and grow your asset base as you build an ever-increasing income stream," by utilizing cash flow strategies designed for low risk with good cash flow, including: writing in-the-money calls, bull call spreads, bull put spreads, index plays, and index spreads.

ON TRACK INVESTING
By David R. Hebert

On Track Investing is the instruction book for novice stock market investors or anyone wanting to practice investment strategies without risking actual cash. Combined with your personal game plan, the Simutrade™ System helps you originate good trades, perfect your timing, and check your open trades against your personal criteria. There are Simutrade™ Worksheets and step by step guides for 10 strategies. On Track Investing helps you develop a step by step map of what exactly you're going to do and how you're going to accomplish it.

ROLLING STOCKS
By Gregory Witt

Rolling Stocks shows you the simplest and most powerful strategy for profiting from the ups and downs of the stock market. You'll learn how to find rolling stocks, get in smoothly at the right price, and time your exit. You will recognize the patterns of rolling stocks and how to make the most money from these strategies. Apply rolling stocks principles to improve your trading options and fortify your portfolio.

SLEEPING LIKE A BABY
By John C. Hudelson

Perhaps the most predominant reason people don't invest in the stock market is fear. *Sleeping Like A Baby* removes the fear from investing and gives you the confidence and knowledge to invest wisely, safely, and profitably.

You'll learn how to build a high quality portfolio and plan for your future and let your investments follow. Begin to invest as early as possible, and use proper asset allocation and diversification to reduce risk.

MAKING A LIVING IN THE STOCK MARKET
By Bob Eldridge

In simplistic, easy to understand terms and presentation, Bob Eldridge will show you how you can change your job and your life by *Making A Living In The Stock Market*. This powerful book is full of real life examples of profitable trades. Pages full of charts, diagrams, and tables help the reader understand how these strategies are implemented.

If you live for your job, have little or no money at the end of each paycheck, and have forgotten your dreams in days gone past, this book is for you. In *Making A Living In The Stock Market*, you can learn how to make money with cash generating strategies including: channeling stock prices, covered calls, selling naked puts, selling naked calls, call (debit) spread, and stock splits.

101 WAYS TO BUY REAL ESTATE WITHOUT CASH
By Wade B. Cook

Wade Cook has personally achieved success after success in real estate. Now, *101 Ways To Buy Real Estate Without Cash* fills the gap left by other authors who have given all the ingredients but not the whole recipe for real estate investing. This is the book for the investor who wants innovative and practical methods for buying real estate with little or no money down.

COOK'S BOOK ON CREATIVE REAL ESTATE
By Wade B. Cook

Make your real estate buying experiences profitable and fun. *Cook's Book On Creative Real Estate* will show you how! You will learn suggestions for finding the right properties, buying them quickly, and profiting ever quicker.

HOW TO PICK UP FORECLOSURES
By Wade B. Cook

Do you want to become an expert moneymaker in real estate? This book will show you how to buy real estate at 60¢ on the dollar or less. You'll learn to find the house before the auction and purchase it with no bank financing–the easy way to millions in real estate. The market for foreclosures is a tremendous place to learn and prosper. *How To Pick Up Foreclosures* takes Wade's methods from Real Estate Money Machine and super charges them by applying the fantastic principles to already-discounted properties.

Owner Financing
By Wade B. Cook

This is a short but invaluable booklet you can give to sellers who hesitate to sell you their property using the owner financing method. Let this pamphlet convince both you and them. The special report, "Why Sellers Should Take Monthly Payments," is included for free!

Real Estate For Real People
By Wade B. Cook

A priceless, comprehensive overview of real estate investing, this book teaches you how to buy the right property for the right price, at the right time. Wade Cook explains all of the strategies you'll need, and gives you 20 reasons why you should start investing in real estate today. Learn how to retire rich with real estate, and have fun doing it.

Real Estate Money Machine
By Wade B. Cook

Wade's first best-selling book reveals the secrets of Wade Cook's own system–the system he earned his first million from. This book teaches you how to make money regardless of the state of the economy. Wade's innovative concepts for investing in real estate not only avoids high interest rates, but avoids banks altogether.

Blueprints for Success, Volume 1
Contributors: Wade Cook, Debbie Losse, Joel Black, Dan Wagner, Tim Semingson, Rich Simmons, Greg Witt, JJ Childers, Keven Hart, Dave Wagner and Steve Wirrick

Blueprints For Success, Volume 1 is a compilation of chapters on building your wealth through your business and making your business function successfully. The chapters cover: education and information gathering, choosing the best business for you from all the different types of business, and a variety of other skills necessary for becoming successful. Your business can't afford to miss out on these powerful insights!

BRILLIANT DEDUCTIONS
By Wade B. Cook

Do you want to make the most of the money you earn? Do you want to have solid tax havens and ways to reduce the taxes you pay? This book is for you! Learn how to get rich in spite of the updated tax laws. See new tax credits, year-end maneuvers, and methods for transferring and controlling your entities. Learn to structure yourself and your family for tax savings and liability protection.

MILLION HEIRS
By John V. Childers, Jr.

In his reader-friendly style, attorney John V. Childers, Jr. explains how you can prepare your loved ones for when you pass away. He explains many details you need to take care of right away, before a death occurs, as well as strategies for your heirs to utilize. Don't leave your loved ones unprepared–get *Millions Heirs*.

THE SECRET MILLIONAIRE GUIDE TO NEVADA CORPORATIONS
By John V. Childers, Jr.

What does it mean to be a secret millionaire? In *The Secret Millionaire Guide To Nevada Corporations*, attorney John V. Childers, Jr. outlines exactly how you can use some of the secret, extraordinary business tactics used by many of today's super-wealthy to protect your assets from the ravages of lawsuits and other destroyers using Nevada Corporations. You'll understand why the state of Nevada has become the preferred jurisdiction for those desiring to establish corporations and how to utilize Nevada Corporations for your financial benefit.

WEALTH 101
By Wade B. Cook

This incredible book brings you 101 strategies for wealth creation and protection that you can't afford to miss. Front to back, it is packed full of tips to supercharge your financial health. If you need to generate more cash flow, this book shows you how through several various avenues. If you are already wealthy, this is the book that will show you strategy upon strategy for minimizing your tax liability and increasing your peace of mind through liability protection.

A+
By Wade B. Cook

A+ is a collection of wisdom, thoughts, and principles of success, which can help you, make millions, even billions of dollars and live an A+ life. As you will see, Wade Cook consistently tries to live his life "in the second mile," to do more than asked, to be above normal.

If you want to live a successful life, you need great role models to follow. For years, Wade Cook's life has been a quest to find successful characteristics of his role models and implement them in his own life. In *A+*, Wade will encourage you to find and incorporate the most successful principles and characteristics of success in your life, too. Don't spend another day living less than an A+ life!

BUSINESS BUY THE BIBLE
By Wade B. Cook

Inspired by the Creator, the Bible truly is the authority for running the business of life. Throughout *Business Buy The Bible,* you are provided with practical advice that helps you apply God's word to your life. You'll learn how you can apply God's word to your life. You'll learn how you can apply God's words to saving, spending and investing, and how you can control debt instead of being controlled by it. You'll also learn how to use God's principles in your daily business activities and prosper.

DON'T SET GOALS (THE OLD WAY)
By Wade B. Cook

Don't Set Goals (The Old Way) will teach you to be a goal-getter, not just a goal-setter. You'll learn that achieving goals is the result of prioritizing and acting. *Don't Set Goals (The Old Way)* shows you how taking action and "paying the price" is more important than simply making the decision to do something. Don't just set goals. Go out and get your goals, go where you want to go!

WADE COOK'S POWER QUOTES, VOLUME 1
By Wade B. Cook

Wade Cook's Power Quotes, Volume 1 is chock full of exciting quotes that have motivated and inspired Mr. Cook. Wade Cook continually asks his students, "To whom are you listening?" He knows that if you get your advice and inspiration from successful people, you'll become successful yourself. He compiled *Wade Cook's Power Quotes, Volume 1* to provide you with a millionaire-on-call when you need advice.

LIVING IN COLOR
By Renae Knapp

Renae Knapp is the leading authority on the Blue Base/Yellow Base Color System and is recognized worldwide for her research and contribution to the study of color. Industries, universities, and men and women around the globe use Renae's tried and true, scientifically-proven system to achieve measurable results.

In *Living In Color*, Renae Knapp teaches you easy to understand methods, which empower you to get more from your life by harnessing the power of color. In an engaging, straightforward way, Renae Knapp teaches the scientific Blue Base/Yellow Base Color System and how to achieve harmony and peace using color. You will develop a mastery of color harmony and an awareness of the amazing role color plays in every area of your life.

Y2K GOLD RUSH
By Wade B. Cook

This book is about how to invest in gold. By reading *Y2K Gold Rush*, you will understand the historical importance of gold. You will learn about the ownership of gold coins and gold stocks, and the benefits of both. You will see that adding gold to your investment portfolio will diversify your assets, safeguard you and your family against catastrophe, and add excitement and profits.

VIDEOS

Dynamic Dollars Video
By Wade B. Cook

Wade Cook's 90-minute introduction to the basics of his Wall Street formulas and strategies. In this presentation designed especially for video, Wade explains the meter drop philosophy, rolling stocks, basics of proxy investing, and writing covered calls. Perfect for anyone looking for a little basic information.

180° Cash Turnaround Video
By Wade B. Cook

Now you know how to make money in any market – up, down, or sideways, if it's moving, you can profit on it! Now spread that knowledge by sharing the 180° Cash Flow Turnaround Seminar on video with your friends, family and co-workers. If you are tired of trying to explain what you are doing in the market, it just takes 180° minutes to turn their stock market thinking around by watching America's premier stock market educator and best selling author Wade B. Cook!

The Wall Street Workshop™ Video Series
By Wade B. Cook

If you can't make it to the Wall Street Workshop™ soon, get a head start with these videos. Ten albums containing 11 hours of intense instruction on rolling stocks, options on stock split companies, writing covered calls, and eight other tested and proven strategies designed to help you increase the value of your investments. By learning, reviewing, and implementing the strategies taught here, you will gain the knowledge and the confidence to take control of your investments, and get your money to work hard for you.

The Next Step Video Series
By Team Wall Street

The advanced version of the Wall Street Workshop™. Full of power-packed strategies from Wade Cook, this is not a duplicate of the Wall

Street Workshop™, but a very important partner. The methods taught in this seminar will supercharge the strategies taught in the Wall Street Workshop™ and teach you even more ways to make more money!

In The Next Step, you'll learn how to find the stocks to fit the formulas through technical analysis, fundamentals, home trading tools, and more.

BUILD PERPETUAL INCOME (BPI)–A VIDEOCASSETTE

Stock Market Institute of Learning™ (Wade Cook Seminars, Inc.) is proud to present Build Perpetual Income, the latest in our ever-expanding series of seminar home study courses. In this video, you will learn powerful real estate cash-flow generating techniques, such as: power negotiating strategies, buying and selling mortgages, writing contracts, finding and buying discount properties, and avoiding debt.

SPREAD & BUTTER™

Spread & Butter™ is Wade Cook's tremendously popular one-day seminar on video. Created in early 1999, this home study course is a live taping of Wade himself teaching his favorite cash flow spread strategies. You will learn everything, from basic Bull Put and Bull Call Spreads to Index Spreads and Calendar Spreads, and how to use each effectively.

CLASSES OFFERED

WEALTH U™

Wealth U™ combines the most powerful, practical and pragmatic training and tools available from Stock Market Institute of Learning, Inc.™, a company that produces more than 30 powerful and effective live and home-study courses. Our education can and does change people's lives, but we have discovered that often newer students are unsure what classes they need most in order to gain the skills necessary for creating, building and protecting net worth.

Wealth U™ is the answer: a comprehensive yet flexible program of core courses, services and tools rolled into one cost-effective package. Wealth U™ is based on a two-fold vision of financial freedom. The key to this vision is in understanding both how to increase income and assets and then how to protect that wealth from the challenges of our economic system. Wealth U™ includes everything you need in order to learn, practice and successfully implement our wealth strategies and reach your dreams!

The first goal is to train our students how to amass enough income-producing assets to comfortably support their chosen lifestyle. Wealth U™ courses look at the complexities of the market from several different angles and provide attendees with strategies to help them make educated and profitable trading decisions. Our market strategies can net substantial gains for the student who is willing to study and apply them. Wealth U™ also includes tools to support our students, from home-study courses for review, to an on-line resource for "watching over the shoulders" of professional traders as they implement our strategies in real trade situations.

Our second goal is to help students understand the vehicles available for protecting their assets and income. With diligent practice and careful planning, trading can become your business. To protect the profits of this new business, Wealth U™'s business classes help students learn to build a new way of life using legal entities such as Nevada corporations, trusts, limited partnerships and more. Wealth U™ students learn how to protect their assets from frivolous lawsuits and excessive taxation.

If you want to be wealthy, this is the place to be.

THE WALL STREET WORKSHOP™
Presented by Wade B. Cook and Team Wall Street
Once you learn the Wade Cook way of trading stocks and options, your time will belong to you again. The Wade Cook way is not really that different from the strategies the wealthy have used for years. However, it is vastly different than what your typical stockbroker or

financial writer will suggest. They want you to turn your money over to a mutual fund manager, broker, or financial planner on the theory that these people know better than you how to take care of your investments.

We believe however, that no one will take better care of your money than you. Treating the stock market as a business means keeping control of your money, getting educated about how the market works and how you can make it work for you. It means making your own decisions, choosing your own investments, and putting the focus on selling.

After attending the Wall Street Workshop™ and applying Wade Cook's system of "Study, Practice, Understand, then Do," you'll be well on your way to achieving your financial goals. You, too, like thousands of other Wall Street Workshop™ graduates, could be making more money than you ever imagined in the stock market–money you can reinvest for more cash flow, or pull out of your brokerage account and spend tomorrow. With a job-free income from the stock market, a life of freedom awaits you and your family. Start your cash flow education today!

BUSINESS ENTITY SKILLS TRAINING (BEST)
Presented by Wade B. Cook and Team Wall Street
This is the initial statement of the B.E.S.T.™ manual, and this one-day seminar is dedicated to teaching new and experienced traders how to do exactly that. You'll learn how to use legal entities such as Nevada corporations, Family Limited Partnerships and Living Trusts. People who are creating wealth through the cash-flow strategies taught in the Wall Street Workshop™ need education on how to protect themselves and their loved ones from the three primary destroyers of financial freedom: lawsuits, income taxes, and death taxes.

Scheduled to follow most Wall Street Workshops™, B.E.S.T.™ is designed to give an overview of basic business entities and correct entity structuring in a one-day format. Your introduction to the world of business entities awaits–it's the B.E.S.T.!

THE NEXT STEP WORKSHOP
Presented by Wade B. Cook and Team Wall Street
Continuing quality education is the key to success, and Stock Market Institute of Learning, Inc., is dedicated to making that education available to you at every step of your journey to financial freedom.

The Next Step™ covers 14 topics in depth-technical analysis training that will let you multiply your returns and dramatically cut losses while you trade the basic Wall Street Workshop™ strategies, plus advanced strategies including Puts, Spreads and Combos.

The information you obtain from this course will dramatically expand your market and financial horizons. By the time you finish the first half of Day One, you'll be too excited to eat! You will learn how to ride the market up, down, and all around, and make money consistently. You will hear how you can limit your risk and harness maximum profits in trade after trade.

YOUTH WALL STREET WORKSHOP
Presented by Team Wall Street
Wade Cook has made a personal commitment to empower the youth of today with desire and knowledge to be self-sufficient. Now you, too, can make a personal commitment to your youth by sending them to the Youth Wall Street Workshop and start your own family dynasty in the process!

Our Youth Wall Street Workshop teaches the power and money making potential of the stock market strategies of the Wall Street Workshop™. The pace is geared to the students, with more time devoted to vocabulary, principles and concepts that may be new to them.

Your children and grandchildren can learn these easy to understand strategies and get that "head start" in life!

If you're considering the Wall Street Workshop™ for the first time, take advantage of our free Youth Wall Street Workshop promotion and bring a son, daughter, or grandchild with you (ages 13 to 18, student, living at home).

Help make your children financially secure in the future by giving them the helping hand in life we all wish we had received.

FINANCIAL CLINIC
Presented by Wade Cook and Team Wall Street

People from all over are making money, lots of money, in the stock market using the proven bread and butter strategies taught by Wade Cook. Is trading in the stock market for you?

Please accept our invitation to come hear for yourself about the amazing money-making strategies we teach. Our Financial Clinic is designed to help you understand how you can learn these proven stock market strategies. In two and one-half short hours you will be introduced to some of the 11 proven strategies we teach at the Wall Street Workshop™. Discover for yourself how they work and how you can use them in your life to get the things you want for you and your family. Come to this introductory event and see what we have to offer. Then make the decision yourself!

EXECUTIVE RETREAT
Presented by Wade B. Cook and Team Wall Street

Many people think that owning and operating a corporation in today's business world is a complicated and overwhelming task. We fail to realize that thousands of small corporations in our country are operating successfully. Incorporation is a powerful tool for protecting wealth from frivolous lawsuits and over-taxation.

The Executive Retreat™ instructors are business entity specialists. This hands-on workshop teaches how to set up, manage, and maintain corporations to maximize the efficiency and impact on your bottom line. This is a unique opportunity for officers of small corporations to network and share information.

WEALTH INSTITUTE
Presented by Wade B. Cook and Team Wall Street

During the three days of the Wealth Institute™, we propose to take you on a journey. The directions will be given in simple, understandable language. Fair warning, though – if you take this journey with us, you may never be the same. Your view of the world of finance will be broader, and your understanding of that world will be deepened and improved.

Our journey will take you easily and inexpensively into the world of entities, step by step. We will explain who should incorporate, why, and most importantly, how. You will learn about the many tax and other benefits available to corporations. We will teach you the structure and strategies of trusts, limited partnerships, and pensions to maximize your net wealth and minimize your tax burdens. We will also look at the importance of and methods for creating positive cash flow.

WHO SHOULD INCORPORATE?

There is simply no other course available anywhere like the Wealth Institute™. If you want to harness the awesome power of legal entities for yourself or your business, the Wealth Institute™ is for you. Typical education is about specialization, focusing on the minute details. At the Wealth Institute™, you'll learn about connections and synergies. You'll discover not just how entities work, but how they work together.

FORTIFY YOUR INCOME

The Fortify Your Income™ seminar (FYI™) is designed to be a refresher course, an additional kick-start to help you use your new knowledge. Our students learn tremendous things at our more basic workshops, but without someone to bounce ideas off of, their interest often wanes (especially if some of their trades don't go as planned). On the other hand, there are students who become excellent traders and want to give something back by sharing what got them to that point.

Don't delay reaching the next level of your success. Making money alone is good, but learning from others and sharing your ideas can be one of the best experiences you can have. Whether you are a novice or a seasoned trader, by the time you leave the FYI you will have had access to knowledge, problems, and solutions to help you face the world of trading head on.

SUPPORT

SUPPORT is designed to be a one-year continuing education program with six one-day events focused on enhancing your knowledge is specific areas. One of the keys to successful trading is to find a strategy and system that fits your personality, available time, money resources, and risk tolerance. There's no better way to design and implement a personal system than to study several until you identify the one that clicks with your lifestyle and trading goals.

SUPPORT is designed as continuing education for graduates of the Wall Street Workshop™ and others who are interested in specialized training in specific strategies. Students can purchase SUPPORT classes separately or pay a low package price for the right the attend multiple classes of your choosing. Focus on one or two favorite strategies or instructors, or explore several to find the right style for your personality and goals!

SEMPER FINANCIAL

Semper Financial Conventions are for everyone! You don't need a financial degree or thousands of dollars to get started making money in the stock market. Anyone who is interested in a brighter financial future for themselves, their spouse, children, friends, church or business associates can come learn these simple cash-flow techniques and formulas in a powerful three-day multi-seminar format.

You owe it to yourself to attend a Semper Financial Investors Educational Convention. Never has there been a more exciting way to continue your education or to inexpensively introduce friends and family to stock market strategies for financial freedom!

Wealth Information Network™ (W.I.N.™)

This subscription Internet service provides you with the latest financial formulas and updated entity structuring strategies. New, timely information is entered Monday through Friday, sometimes four or five times a day. Wade Cook and his Team Wall Street staff write for W.I.N.™, giving you updates on their own current stock plays, companies who announced earnings, companies who announced stock splits, and the latest trends in the market.

W.I.N.™ is also divided into categories according to specific strategies and contains archives of all our trades so you can view our history. If you are just getting started in the stock market, this is a great way to follow people who are doubling some of their money every $2^1/_2$ to 4 months. If you are experienced already, it's the way to confirm your research with others who are generating wealth through the stock market.

IQ Pager™

This is a system which beeps you as events and announcements are made on Wall Street. With IQ Pager™, you'll receive information about events like major stock split announcements, earnings surprises, important mergers and acquisitions, judgements or court decisions involving big companies, important bankruptcy announcements, big winners and losers, and disasters. If you're getting your financial information from the evening news, you're getting it too late. The key to the stock market is timing. Especially when you're trading in options, you need up-to-the-minute (or second) information. You cannot afford to sit at a computer all day looking for news or wait for your broker to call. IQ Pager™ is the ideal partner to the Wealth Information Network™ (W.I.N.™).

The Incorporation Handbook
By Wade B. Cook

Incorporation made easy! This handbook tells you who, why, and, most importantly, how to incorporate. Included are samples of the ctlforms you will use when you incorporate, as well as a step-by-step guide from the experts.

TRAVEL AGENT INFORMATION

The only sensible solution for the frequent traveler. This kit includes all of the information and training you need to be an outside travel agent for a stable company. There are no hassles, no requirements, no forms or restrictions, just all the benefits of traveling for substantially less every time.

EXPLANATIONS NEWSLETTER

In the wild and crazy stock market game, *EXPLANATIONS* Newsletter will keep you on your toes! Every month you'll receive coaching, instruction and encouragement with engaging articles designed to bring your trading skills to a higher level. Learn new twists on Wade's 13 basic strategies, find out about beneficial research tools, read reviews on the latest investment products and services, and get detailed answers to your trading questions. With *EXPLANATIONS*, you'll learn to be your own best asset in the stock market game and stay on track to a rapidly growing portfolio! Continue your education as an investor and subscribe today!